Systems in Teaching
and Learning

THE PROFESSIONAL EDUCATION SERIES

Walter K. Beggs, *Editor*
Dean Emeritus
Teachers College
University of Nebraska

Royce H. Knapp, *Research Editor*
Regents Professor of Education
Teachers College
University of Nebraska

Systems in Teaching and Learning

by

ROBERT FILBECK

Professor of Educational
Psychology and Measurements
University of Nebraska

PROFESSIONAL EDUCATORS PUBLICATIONS, INC.
LINCOLN, NEBRASKA

Library of Congress Catalog Card No.: 72-94971

ISBN   0-88224-024-2

Contents

CHAPTER 1

Individualization of Instruction

Despite present-day demands for education to be "individual-ized," there is really nothing new about the idea. Educators have long recognized that grouping learners into classes is simply an expedient, and an economic expedient at that. It is no secret that *individuals* learn, not groups. Some learnings may occur only in a group setting, or with greater efficiency in groups, and some individuals *prefer* to learn in a group context, but it is the behavior of individuals which changes (thus permitting an inference that "learning" has taken place).[1] The group's behavior will change only as a function of changes in the behavior of individuals.

If instruction is considered as occurring in many places in addi-tion to schools and other formal settings, and as consisting of *all* activities designed to assist humans to become more proficient and content in coping with their life problems, then it is apparent that the vast majority of the instruction which takes place in the world is individual in nature.

Why then the concern about individualizing even further?

Obviously it is important to be economical and efficient in the operation of our schools, but our group-centered processes have, all too often, compromised many educational qualities. Instruction for *learning by all students* has taken a back seat to a process of *group management*. The group approach tends to direct the attention and concerns of teachers to the entire class, to a presumed "average," and above all to course *content* rather than to individual learnings, po-tentials, and desires. As a consequence, many, if not most, students learn considerably less than they are able, forget more than is neces-sary, require more time for mastery than is necessary, often experience little joy in learning, and evaluate the majority of their formal learn-ing experiences as "irrelevant."

This indictment of group-centered classes holds despite the ef-forts of good teachers to provide individual students with personal assistance at times of need. *Need* is usually defined in terms of a deviation from group norms, and assistance is usually in the direction of returning the deviant individual to full group membership rather than achievement of idiosyncratic goals.

The indictment also holds despite the fact that our techniques for conducting group instruction have reached a point of "high art."

Recent social concerns about respect for the rights of students as individuals, with greater powers of self-determination and self-responsibility for behavior, have revealed, in sharp contrast, the deleterious effects of group-centered approaches, regardless of how efficient they may be. Certainly, the group approach vitiates much self-determination and assumption of responsibility for one's own learning.

While educational *practices* have emphasized group-centered approaches, the *concept* of individualized approaches has appeared frequently in educational literature. The testing movement, with all its limitations and possible evils, has constantly reminded educators of the extent of diversity among students. This awareness has probably been responsible for keeping the notion of individualization of education alive, to the extent that it continues to be written about and talked about, even if not, in reality, practiced.

The testing movement, beginning with the early Binet scales for identification of learning deficits, was instrumental in establishing limited attempts to individualize, characterized as "special education," "compensatory education," the various "track systems," "special enrichment classes," and so on. No doubt, these efforts to reduce the *range* of individual differences within groups have some potential for the individualizing of instruction, but they also tend to restrict opportunities for learning from diverse peers and thus are dropping from favor.

The testing movement, while encouraging the establishment of the grouping of students according to their real or supposed differences, also revealed the inadequacy of any *single strategy* for grouping. If students are grouped according to ability (IQ), the resultant groups differ as much as previous groupings in terms of interests, reading levels, learning styles, socioeconomic status, and special talents. In fact, there is no way to group that reduces individual differences to the point where all members of a class will respond equally to a given learning experience.

The testing movement, by the very nature of the data it produces, cannot do more than *identify* a problem. Test scores, ratings, and similar criteria *describe* individuals or a group as they are at a point in time. Measurement information tends to "suggest" only that heterogeneity be reduced by differential grouping, but "suggests" nothing about how learning or behavior change from that point will take place.

The quest for a means to truly individualize instruction, necessitated by awareness of the individual rights of students and the vast array of differences among them, must, therefore, include a search for a new *technology* of instruction. This in turn must be based on a science of the learning process which isolates, identifies, and determines the functional arrangement of variables and events with the learning process. Measurement data from standardized tests, which describe learners as they are, are not likely to identify these factors, so a technology of instruction must be derived from another branch of the behavioral sciences: namely from learning research.[2]

RESEARCH IN LEARNING PROCESS: A SCIENCE FOR THE DEVELOPMENT OF AN INSTRUCTIONAL TECHNOLOGY

Learning and instructional research has, over the past thirty years, provided an empirical basis for formulating many scientific principles or "laws," which are *all* potentially important to consider when designing learning experiences. However, the author has identified twelve, which, if rigorously employed, will suffice as a basis for developing an entirely adequate technology for individualized instruction.[3]

For each of the twelve principles, the author has included: (1) an initial statement of the principle, (2) an example of the principle "in action," and (3) a brief statement of the implications for instructional technology.

Principal One

Learning research has consistently shown that new responses are repeated as a function of the consequences of those responses. If the consequences are pleasurable, the learner tends to continue making the response to maintain the pleasurable consequences. This is termed a *positive reinforcer*, since it tends to increase the rate of responding. Other consequences of behavior are less pleasurable, and the learner tends to act in ways to reduce the discomfort, either by withholding the response that leads to unpleasant consequences or by engaging in other behaviors. Presumably, the *avoidance or escape from* aversive consequences is reinforcing since the avoidant or escape behavior tends to be maintained. These are termed *negative reinforcers* or *punishers*, and the process inferred to occur is often called *negative reinforcement.*

Regardless of the type of reinforcement used, it has been consistently shown that consequences, to be effective, must be apparent to the learner almost immediately after he makes the response to be learned. However, after a number of immediate reinforcers have been presented, responses will be maintained if the schedule shifts to a ratio of one reinforcer per five, ten, or even more responses. It appears that a stronger response pattern is established if the schedule for ratio reinforcement is made a variable ratio, first reinforcing each response, then every other one, then every third one, then (perhaps) reinforcing on a random schedule.

Postive reinforcers may be basic or *primary* (such as food when hungry or water when thirsty), or *secondary* (such as money tokens, approval of peers, affection, and "feedback" of success). Secondary reinforcers are *learned* as a result, probably, of having been associated with primary reinforcers in early developmental experiences. By the time a child reaches school, he typically is responding largely for secondary or learned reinforcers, although M & M's, peanuts, Kool-Aid, and other foods will still reinforce learning. By far, the most useful learned positive reinforcer for school learning is *feedback*, or knowledge of success or correct responding. Much success has been reported when checkmarks or other "tokens" are awarded students for making appropriate responses.[4] By and large, there appears to be little utility for schools in the use of negative reinforcers. The effects are too unpredictable. Often, under a system utilizing negative reinforcers, we find learners making emotional responses (withdrawal or "dropping out," avoidance, and even aggressive responses) and failing to learn appropriate responses.

The implications of research in reinforcement for developing a technology of individualized instruction would seem to be:

1. Provision must be made to provide positive feedback of success or correct responding very frequently at first and on a random basis later in the learning experience.
2. Learning experiences must be *active* rather than quiet sitting and listening. Reinforcement can only function when active responding occurs.
3. Learning experiences should be designed to assure that every learner makes a very high percentage of correct responses.

Feedback of "wrong responding" amounts to a negative reinforcer for most learners, and they will tend to avoid or escape (or even aggress against) the learning situation.

4. Learning experiences must be designed to use *existing* secondary reinforcers. Persons differ in their patterns of development and so have different patterns of secondary reinforcers. The design of learning experiences should provide a choice or "menu" of reinforcers and an opportunity for learners to select their reinforcer for the day. Their present reinforcers should be paired or associated with copious feedback to develop this type of reinforcer. In effect, the extensive development of feedback as a reinforcer may be identical to developing "an *interest*" in a subject or an activity.

Principle Two

Behavior is not only under the control of consequences, it is also under the influence of antecedent conditions or *cues*. We are never certain just which few stimuli from a rich field of stimuli function as cues for behavior, but in the school there are many that can be identified with some certainty: printed words, pictures, verbal communications, teacher mannerisms, peer behaviors, and so forth. Certainty about the influence of antecedent stimuli increases if they are manipulated or changed and observations are made as to what behaviors then change.

We know, for example, that learning is made more efficient if objectives are stated clearly before a learning experience—that is, if statements of objectives clearly describe what a learner *will be able to do* after completing the learning experience.

It is necessary to shield some learners from "distracting" cues—that is, cues for inappropriate behavior. Some students have learned so many responses to cues presented by peers that they cannot "attend" to the cues for cognitive behaviors, so initial learning experiences must be designed to reduce the cues from fellow learners. As learner behavior comes under the control of cues made to "stand out" from the surroundings—for example, by clear statements of objectives or through reducing the number of distractor cues—the deliberately "highlighted" cues can be faded or made less obvious. The "naturally occurring" cues within the setting will then take over the role of influencing behavior, presumably by a process of having been associated with the highlighted cues. For example, a teacher may provide highlighted cues in the form of study questions that direct a student's attention to significant points in his reading assignments. The questions can be faded gradually to the point that occasional subheadings will cue students to the appropriate attending behavior. The chapter subheadings may serve as cues for learners to construct their own questions and thus make their reading "meaningful," "purposeful," and even "relevant."

As will become apparent in the discussion of the principles that follow, the form of cueing provided students determines, to very great degree, what behavior changes take place in a learning experience.

Principle Three

Behavior elicited by certain cues will diminish or be reduced in frequency if it is not reinforced. This process of *extinction* probably accounts for some of the losses of learning commonly referred to as "forgetting."[5] Since schools are interested in long-term retention, it is important for newly learned material or new skills to be rehearsed or repeated a number of times under conditions of reinforcement. By shifting to variable schedules of reinforcement, the extinction process will be slowed. Perhaps the most appropriate means to reduce extinction effects is to emphasize learnings which are *useful* to the learner in the world outside the classroom. As learned behaviors are used in solving real-life problems, they are reinforced by *feedback of successful problem-solving* and rewarded by recognition of peers, and even, perhaps, by *increased income, job status, and acclaim.*

Principle Four

Learning that occurs as a response to a *limited* array of cues will transfer to a limited extent to other situations. Teachers have long been puzzled as to why students who make "perfect" responses to verbal cues on a test fail to make the same responses to cues in the real world—that is, why they do not "apply" what they have learned. The excuse is frequently made that students do not "want" to apply what they have learned, that it is a matter of motivation. In many cases, it is more a matter of failure by teachers to provide learning experiences that incorporate cues identical or similar to the cues present in the real world. Teachers are often "hung-up" on verbal-symbolic learning and fail to recognize that such learning does not transfer well.

The teacher who plans to individualize instruction will find it necessary to provide a cue environment that approximates the one in which learnings are to be used. This suggests liberal use of various simulation devices, which can replicate natural cues and even gradually introduce additional cues to build up abilities to respond to very complex arrays of cues. Pictures, diagrams, films, tape-recordings, models, dramatizations, sociodramas, and educational games are all media for replicating cue situations as a means to enhance transfer of learning.

Principle Five

While it is necessary to deliberately include experiences to increase transfer on generalization, some learnings will generalize in appropriate ways. Some children will make *word reversals:* for example, reading *saw* when given the cue of *was.* Others respond to teachers in ways they have learned as appropriate for responding to other adults (parents, police, baby sitters, etc.). They have not learned to discriminate among the various cues they perceive. *Discrimination learnings* (along with generalizations) represent the basis for most of the so-called higher-level learnings that represent educational objectives and goals. Most complex analytic and synthesizing, or integrating, abilities are built up from chains of generalized and discriminated learnings.

In developing individualized instructional experiences, the teacher must be able to analyze the overall goals to determine which discrimination learnings are likely to require extensive practice under conditions of reinforcement before becoming established as a part of the learner's repertory. Liberal use of positive and negative *examples* or *instances* and directed observations of real-life events seem to be imperative inclusions in learning experiences for developing discrimination abilities. Development of precise, technical vocabularies also appears to aid in developing the ability to respond appropriately in complex social and work-related situations.

Principle Six

Learner *set,* or *intent,* will influence the attention and perseverance of students as they progress through learning experiences. Set, or intention, is an inferred mental state assumed to exist prior to emission of certain behaviors. In reality, these terms refer to the behaviors themselves, which may be categorized under the headings of "attentive," "interested," "concentration," "stick-to-itiveness." It has been empirically determined that set will probably occur if the first step in a learning experience indicates to a student: (1) in a general way what he will be mastering; (2) how he will be able to make use of the skills and understandings he is learning; (3) how the new learnings complement, supplement, or integrate with prior learning; (4) the procedures he may follow in achieving objectives; and (5) what immediate rewards and reinforcements are available for learning. In other words, student behavior will be attentive, interested, etc. This first step is often referred to as an *advance organizer*. As such, it functions as a very complex cue for behaviors that are important for learning to occur.

(Note: After completing this and the next chapter, the reader might devote a few minutes to evaluating them as an "advance organizer" for the book.)

Principle Seven

Learning tasks which are divided into small, discrete steps, with reinforcement (feedback) being provided for completion of each step, appear to be helpful to most learners. Programmed texts apply this principle, being built up of substantial numbers of small learning tasks called *frames*. Each time a learner responds to a frame, he is *immediately* informed of the correctness of his response.

This is not to be taken as advocacy of programmed instruction as the basis for individualized instruction, although it may well have a place in any individualized instructional program. Rather, it is a principle which dictates that teachers should become skilled in developing learning experiences in *bits*, with each bit providing practice or rehearsal experiences with feedback. The skill of providing feedback experiences is critical. Obviously, time-honored paper-and-pencil tests have only limited feedback value if one is concerned about transfer and application abilities. Teachers will need to develop other types of exercises that will permit learners to demonstrate their new abilities to themselves and others.

Principle Eight

The need to reduce complex learnings to small steps is reduced if the complex behavior can be *modeled*. There is ample evidence that children learn critical social skills, psychomotor skills, and many verbal skills through a process of observing someone else demonstrate a behavior and then being reinforced for emitting similar behavior. Thus, if a child observes a parent go through a complex sequence of greeting a guest, taking his coat and hat, inviting him to be seated, and offering him refreshments, then sees the guest smile, talk to the parent, relax, and say pleasant, complimentary things, the child is likely to emulate the parent's behavior. Likewise a student who sees a movie that portrays a worker setting up a machine lathe, then succeeding in turning out a complex machine part, will tend to duplicate the movements and decisions made by the filmed worker. Note that in each case there is an opportunity to observe the *effects* or *consequences* of appropriate behavior—in other words, to see that reinforcing feedback is forthcoming for certain responses. Cue learning and reinforcement effects apparently can occur as a *vicarious* experience from observing a film, or from seeing a play or a series of pictures or diagrams.

The educator, to develop experiences for individual learners, must develop the ability to design and evaluate the effects of demonstrations and other observational experiences that include feedback for correct responding.

Principle Nine

Higher-level learnings, or *problem-solving skills,* are complex behaviors built up as a composite of basic, more simple skills. A process of analysis of complex learnings will reveal the underlying component skills. If the teacher's goal (or the student's, for that matter) is to become proficient in a complex skill, the procedure to follow is to arrange *small-step learnings,* using a process of analysis to identify the functional bits of knowledge or skill included in the complex skill. Design of demonstrations or other modeling procedures should be based on a prior analysis in order to clearly illustrate the component learnings involved in complex skills.

The implications for teachers are obvious. They will need to: (1) develop skills in formulating instructional goals in terms of outcomes, which are definable by reference to complex *behaviors* (rather than in terms of ability to "think," ability to "reason," or other concepts of equal ambiguity or fuzziness), and (2) develop skills in analyzing and breaking down complex behaviors into simpler learnings, which may then be *combined* into complex skills and understandings.

Principle Ten

Learning tends to be most rapid, efficient, and pleasurable when students are provided information that they are becoming progressively more competent in complex problem-solving skills.

This principle suggests that teachers should become skilled in sequencing learning experiences from simple to complex and able to design successive experiences to include prior learnings in combination with newer learnings.

Principle Eleven

Learners vary in the rate at which they develop understandings and skills, some progressing rapidly, others much more slowly. An individual learner will vary from one day to another and from one subject to another. The variations in learning rate are not always predictable. IQ test results, analyses of cognitive style, and measures of differential interests or attitudes towards learning do not account for significant amounts of such variation in learning. Some of the variation is best explained in terms of variability in prior learnings. Students who have not mastered prerequisite learnings do not learn new material as speedily as those who have.

Principle Twelve

With preparation, learners can develop the ability to organize their own learning experiences, provide cues for their own behavior, and reinforce themselves for correct responding. In a very real sense, learners can become self-teachers.

In developing individualized instructional programs, teachers may progressively involve learners in the design of increasingly larger portions of their own learning experiences. A significant portion of their understandings and skills will then be in an area we might refer to as *self-management*. With repeated experiences in self-management, which schools can provide through multiple learning experiences, this complex cluster of skills should readily generalize to the larger life space of the individual. Generalized self-management skills may represent the ultimate extent of the problem-solving skills that can be provided by the schools. This is apparent if constant readjustment to life situations and development of new coping skills through modification of one's own behavior is seen as the inevitable requirement placed on man by life.

The teacher developing individualized learning experiences must include provisions for learners to progress at differing rates. Provision should also be made to permit learners to begin an experience at points consistent with their prior learnings.

If nothing else, the foregoing twelve principles and their corollaries reveal that the task of preparing for individualized instruction is *extremely complex*. It involves a great many distinct steps, many of which are interrelated in the sense that some steps are dependent upon other steps having been completed first.

It is also apparent that individualized instruction will require that *materials* do much of the work presently considered to be the responsibility of the teacher. Thirty students, for example, will not all be ready at the same time to learn from a demonstration. Nor can a teacher repeat the same demonstration thirty times if anything else is to be accomplished.

The requirement for materials prepared in conformity with the twelve principles requires that teachers become much more proficient and exacting as *planners*. Materials must be designed to accomplish a particular purpose. Study assignments in typical texts, even when accompanied by workbooks, will seldom conform to more than one or two of the twelve principles. The teacher must become proficient in analyzing, revising, and creating materials, arranging them in learnable bits and in proper sequences to actualize the principles of learning and instruction.

Fortunately, within the past few decades a technology has developed which improves man's ability to plan complex activities very effectively. It can be adapted into a technology for developing instructional techniques or for adapting already developed techniques to achieve the purposes of individualized instruction.

This technology is commonly referred to as the *systems approach*. It represents a complex body of skills, all having one objective: to produce instructional materials that conform to what is known about learning and instruction and are effective with a wide range of individual learners.

CHAPTER 2

Systems and the Systems Approach:
A Technology for Planning

MEANING OF "SYSTEM"

System is a familiar term. Everybody, at one time or another, uses it. As with any term in common use over an extended period, it has tended to become rather loose and has acquired additional meanings (sometimes including emotionalized connotations). Since the term has by now become imprecise and actually means very little, it is necessary to clarify and make more precise the concept of system as it is applied to individualized instruction.[1]

Concept of Systems

In its most general form, a system may be either an object or an event. The object or event, however, must be divisible into separate parts or phases, and the entire assemblage of parts or phases should function (more or less) in synchrony.

From the definition thus far, almost all aspects of life can be classed as systems. Most objects in man's environment are made up of different components or elements, which are interrelated in one way or another.

To make the meaning even more precise, it should be added that the functional relationship *exists for a purpose*: to permit sequential transformation of raw materials into products or services. Thus, a system is more than an assemblage of parts — it must serve some end.

Under this definition the following objects can be classed as systems: (1) an electric fuse, (2) a door latch, (3) a typewriter, (4) a tape-recorder, (5) an automobile, (6) a jet airliner, and (7) the Bell Telephone Company. Each of these represents an aggregation of separate parts. Each part has a distinctive function to perform, and there are interrelations among the parts. In each case, the relationship is determined by the overall function (purpose) of the system.

Now consider whether the following represent systems as defined here: (1) a single body cell, (2) the heart, (3) a rose bush, (4) an ant colony, (5) a tidal marsh,[2] (6) the oceans, (7) the earth, and (8) the sun and planets. The answer is yes, these too are systems. The question of "purpose" in the metaphysical sense is not always apparent, but it is possible to define *effects* of the operation of each system and to assume that these represent the intention or purpose of the system.

In the foregoing lists of examples, two general types of systems are apparent: *man-made* systems, which are devised by man for his purposes, and *natural* systems, for which the ultimate purpose is not clear. The concern in this book is with man-made systems only, so further consideration will not be given to natural systems.

Each example of a man-made system given in the first list possesses physical, tangible properties. Consider now the following: (1) a procedure for starting an automobile; (2) a procedure for staggering lunch periods for one thousand students in a lunch room that seats two hundred; (3) a procedure for routing city buses to serve the maximum number of patrons while traveling the fewest miles; (4) a procedure for preparing meals for a family; and (5) a procedure for locating a defective transistor in a color television set.

These too represent systems, although the components are not joined or physically linked as in the case of the previous examples. Since the separate parts often include action by a person and a machine, appliance, or other material object, the total system becomes a *man-machine* system. For example, a typist plus a typewriter plus a dictaphone becomes a man-machine "document-reproduction system."

Note in these latter examples of systems that the system components consist partially of *procedures* or *steps* in an overall plan. Each step or process has its unique function to perform as one aspect of overall system function. The process of planning a curriculum or educational program then may be a system.

Systems, Subsystems, and Suprasystems

Thus far, the concept of system has been defined only in the conjunctive sense—that is, by identifying major *attributes* of a generalized systems model. In actual usage, a system is defined in a relational sense. A closer analysis shows that system *parts* are themselves systems. Each part can be further divided into smaller elements, each of which has its own function and its own relationship to other components. Thus, it can be said that systems are made up of *subsystems*.

Further analysis will easily show that any system under study exists as a subsystem to a still larger system, which might be termed a *suprasystem*. Consider the following:

1. The entire human society constitutes a system.
2. Societies can be analyzed to identify a number of *institutions*, such as the family, education, law enforcement, etc., each of which functions as a system.
3. Each institution can be analyzed to identify functional components (for example, educational institution comprises preschool, elementary, secondary, postsecondary, etc.). Each component functions as a system.
4. Each functional component can be analyzed to identify elements (each component of educational institution contains instructional, administrative, pupil services, housing, transportation, financial, and other elements). The elements each function as a complete system.
5. If the elements are further divided, it will be found that the product of each division will also meet the definitional criteria for a system.

Now, which is system, which is subsystem, and which is suprasystem? It depends, of course, on where one happens to be standing. If the view is from the position of studying the instructional system, then the educational system becomes the suprasystem, and the various subjects in the curriculum, the instructional personnel, the materials, and the equipment all become subsystems. Use of the term *system* is governed by convention. It is used to designate the particular functional conglomerate under consideration at the moment. The system being considered today may become the suprasystem that includes the subsystem to be examined as a system tomorrow.

In all cases, however, analysis will indicate that any system receives inputs from a suprasystem in the form of raw materials and energy (or resources) and returns finished products or services to the suprasystem. Goals and purposes for systems, then, flow from suprasystems. It is reasonable to assume that if (or when) a system becomes dysfunctional—that is, does not accept the inputs from the suprasystem, or does not transform them in ways which result in useful "outputs" (products or services)—it will be eliminated, replaced, or modified, lest functioning of the suprasystem be impaired.

At this point it will be helpful to summarize the discussion of system in the form of a diagram. Fig. 2.1 has been prepared as a "model," or two-dimensional representation, of a system. The system

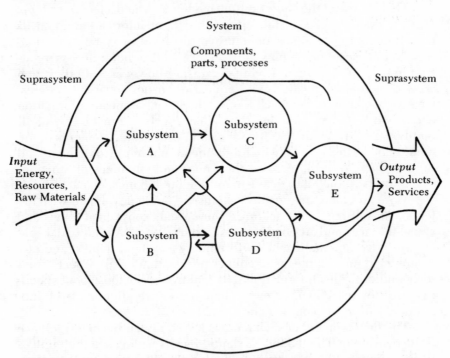

Fig. 2.1. General System Model

is represented as the large circle, and it is shown receiving inputs from the suprasystem and discharging outputs into the same suprasystem. In actuality, of course, the outputs go to other *peer systems*, which comprise the suprasystem. Subsystems in the model are depicted as smaller circles with connecting arrows. The arrows indicate that two or more subsystems are functionally related, with the output of one being received as input by another.

The functional relationship of subsystem *B* to subsystem *D* is more complex, as indicated by the two arrows indicating a flow going in both directions. This relationship is best illustrated by an example. Suppose subsystem *B* is, in actuality, the administrative operations of a large school district and subsystem *D* comprises all the libraries in that system. The administrative subsystem supplies budget, procedural regulations, personnel, and so forth to the libraries. The libraries, in turn, provide the administration with data on which to base decisions: student reading preferences, staff work-loads, class demands of libraries, and so on, all necessary information for the making of administrative decisions.

This feature of the model system has been termed a *feedback loop.* It is an example of a system utilizing data or information about its own functioning to adjust or improve the level of system functioning. Not all systems employ this feature so it is not a necessary attribute of system as such. Living organisms, however, with their rich array of neural connections and endocrine or hormonal subsystems, have very elaborate feedback loops, which communicate information about bodily functioning and thus affect levels of functioning of all bodily parts. Muscular activity, for example, activates elements of the neural-endocrine system, which provide neural impulses to heart and lungs, which, in turn, increase their rates and efficiency of functioning, to prepare the total organism for heightened muscular activity.

More and more man-made systems are being developed with the feedback, self-regulatory feature. Thermostats sense heat levels and signal furnaces and air-conditioners to start or stop. An industrial concern or governmental agency will employ a systems analyst and buy computer time as a means to collect information on all aspects of all its operations. This information will "control" decisions about speeding up, slowing down, or even changing entire alignments of subsystems within the company or agency.

The development of such feedback systems has become a science in its own right. The reader, no doubt, recalls having seen references to the science of *cybernetics.* Research in cybernetics will become increasingly important to educators as they begin to develop instructional systems and thus need to systematically assemble the data that will enable them to adjust the systems.

SYSTEMS APPROACH: SYSTEMS ANALYSIS, SYSTEMS SYNTHESIS

From the foregoing analysis of the *notion* of system, a *systems concept* has emerged for the reader. As this concept is used and applied, it will gradually become integrated into a *systems view.* This view, which may be defined as a habitual manner of examining the events of life, evolves into the *systems approach.* The systems approach involves the processes of analyzing systems, developing (synthesizing) systems, and finding and testing solutions to problems.

This progression has been portrayed in diagrammatic form in Fig. 2.2.[3] Note the feedback line in Fig. 2.2. This indicates that as one has experiences in systems analysis, systems synthesis, and systematic problem-solving, his previously developed notions of system, systems concept, and systems view will be modified or adjusted to the new realities represented by each experience. The next section of this chapter provides the basis for experiences that will provide the reader with a type of feedback data, leading to modification of the concepts, views, and approaches he has developed as a result of reading the preceding sections.

Systems Analysis

As was indicated above, mankind is literally surrounded by systems. At times, some will malfunction or there will be reason to believe that a particular system no longer functions for the larger suprasystem. It then becomes necessary to redesign or restructure the existing system. In a similar vein, advances in technology may lead to the conclusion that an existing system is not as efficient as it could be and needs to be overhauled to take advantage of the new technology. (Consider, for example, the changes made possible in instructional systems by the development of the movie projector.)

From a systems viewpoint, such changes should not be made willy-nilly or in an arbitrary fashion. They should be preceded by a *system analysis*, a process of first identifying the functional components or subsystems, then defining the interrelationships of the components. Often an entire system can be represented by a complex mathematical formula, which describes quantitatively both what happens to materials at each step of a process and the conditions, rate of flow, and other factors that characterize the process at each point.

With information derived from such an analysis, it is possible to determine much more precisely the part or process one should modify and the kind of modification that is necessary, and to predict the effects of the modification on overall system functioning.

Systems analysis is a useful tool. With today's highspeed computers, a team of systems analysts can develop mathematical models for extremely complex operations. Such models permit managers and planning specialists to correct operational problems or incorporate new technology in effective, efficient ways. Systems analysis procedures are essential, for example, to effect Program Planning and Budgeting Systems (PPBS) as one means to more rationally allocate school monies and other resources.

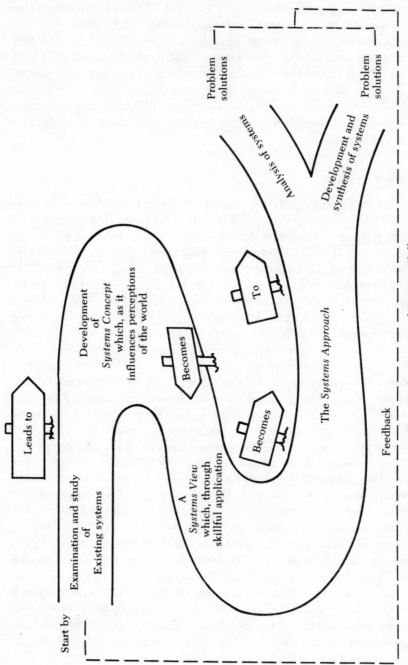

Fig. 2.2. Progression of Systems Skills

Note that the entire process of system analysis is related to improvement of system attainment of output goals. The analysis has meaning *only* as it relates processes to outcome. It does more than simply *describe* an operational system; the analysis defines the *contribution* of components to total system functioning.

Systems Synthesis

Not only is man surrounded by systems that require frequent or even ongoing analysis, he is constantly developing or *synthesizing* new systems. Most inventions are synthesized systems, as are new governmental programs, such as the "war on poverty."

A new system is called into being when the suprasystem has a need for a new function—that is, a new product or service. The need is defined, and satisfaction of that need represents the goals for the new system. The inputs are defined (raw materials, energy, etc.) and successive steps in the transformation of raw materials to product are identified. A subsystem is then designed to function at each step of the transformation process. The assembly of subsystems into an operational whole represents the final step in system building.

Note the critical step of *goal definition* in systems synthesis. The development of a system is entirely controlled by the goals established for it. The goal is analyzed to determine the specific objectives that must be accomplished along the way to achieve the goal. The specific objectives then control the processes that make up the subsystems.

Problem-Solving

As indicated above, systems are analyzed and synthesized as means to *solve problems*. Mankind's existence consists of solving one problem after another. Man modifies himself and his environment in ways he predicts will provide him with greater satisfactions or with fewer dissatisfactions. Many of man's efforts at problem-solving are random, trial-and-error. If an effort proves to be erroneous, he seldom performs an analysis to identify where it was wrong. He either discards the effort or continues it, accepting the error.

Seldom in history has man *systematically* synthesized systems as means to solve problems. If he had, very likely fewer errors would have been made. The systems approach, by first clearly defining desired outcomes and goals as projected solutions, permits one to use available knowledge and technology in the most expeditious ways and thereby reduces the amount of error. Obviously, there is not always going to be an available technology or process for every objective. However, where objectives are clearly identified, the process of creating or inventing processes is considerably simplified, as will become apparent in subsequent chapters of this book.

The systems approach, then, is a system for the development of systems for solving problems. As a system, it can be portrayed as a model or in schematic form. Fig. 2.3 is a schematic representation of a system for problem-solving.

Fig. 2.3 is deemed to be largely self-explanatory. One or two special mentions should be made, however.

1. Note that explicit provision has been made for developing a feedback loop by including a process for developing measures to be used in determining whether or not objectives are achieved. In most man-made systems this is an imperative step. Most man-made systems are *probabilistic* systems. One can predict the effects of most processes only within the limits of probability. Very few processes work perfectly, 100 percent of the time. Some processes, predicted to be successful, work not at all. Feedback is necessary to detect such departures from predictions. If one were developing a *deterministic* system (such as a door latch or other mechanical device), a feedback loop would not be useful.
2. The final step should be interpreted as indicating that systems for developing systems must provide for feedback, as do the systems developed by the approach. In other words, the development process must be evaluated as a basis for further learning about system development.

SYSTEMS APPROACH TO DEVELOPING INSTRUCTIONAL MATERIALS

At the close of Chapter 1, it was indicated that individualization of instruction requires the development of large amounts of special materials. These materials must conform to a number of principles of learning and instruction if they are to be effective. It was pointed out that the materials now available do not conform to these principles and so must be modified: added to or supplemented by teacher-developed materials.

This lack of materials constitutes a problem. If the process of individualized instruction is conceptualized as a system with

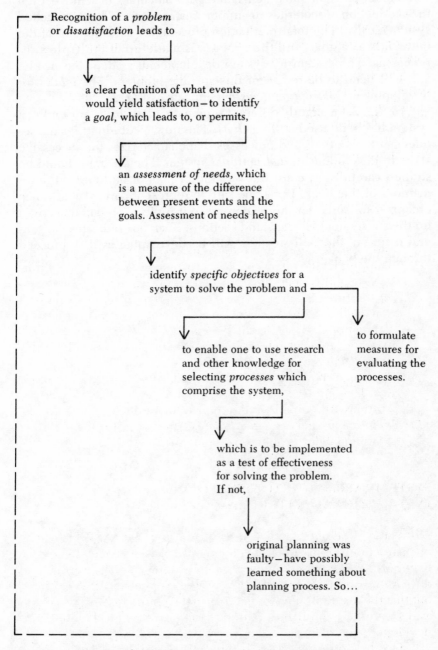

Recognition of a *problem* or *dissatisfaction* leads to

a clear definition of what events would yield satisfaction – to identify a *goal*, which leads to, or permits,

an *assessment of needs*, which is a measure of the difference between present events and the goals. Assessment of needs helps

identify *specific objectives* for a system to solve the problem and

to enable one to use research and other knowledge for selecting *processes* which comprise the system,

to formulate measures for evaluating the processes.

which is to be implemented as a test of effectiveness for solving the problem. If not,

original planning was faulty – have possibly learned something about planning process. So...

Fig. 2.3. The Systems Approach: A System for Employing Systems Technology for Problem-solving

component parts, or subsystems, and with outcomes to achieve, then the production of materials to support instruction can be approached systematically. The total production process has development of the materials as a goal, and the process is made up of multiple sub-processes. The system for system development, as depicted in Fig. 2.3, will need to be recast for this specific problem. The model for developing an *instructional system* appears as Fig. 2.4.

In Fig. 2.4 a slightly different schematic mode for representing a system has been used: a *flow chart*. The flow chart identifies the sequence of operations and processes that characterizes the successive steps in developing an *instructional* system. The diagram should be studied carefully. It constitutes a kind of plan or outline for the remainder of this book. It may be said to represent part of an advance organizer (of sorts) for the reader, since it indicates broad objectives for the subsequent chapters and sections. Each box indicates the general nature of the skills readers will be developing as they proceed through the book.

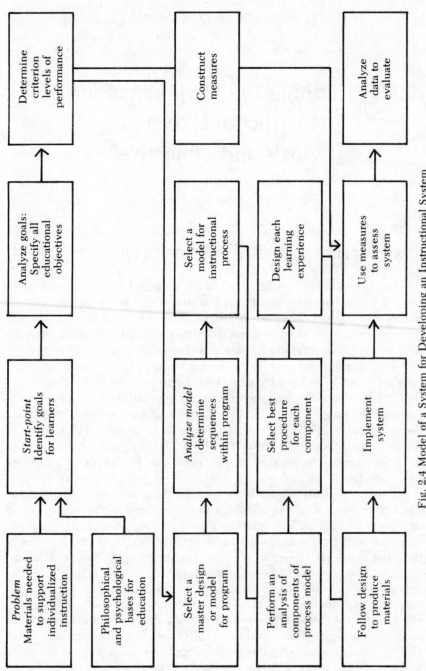

Fig. 2.4 Model of a System for Developing an Instructional System

CHAPTER 3

Defining the Purposes of an
Instructional System:
Goals and Objectives

GOAL SETTING: A NECESSARY FIRST STEP

In this chapter, readers will be introduced to procedures comprising the subsystem for defining instructional goals and objectives. Some of the procedures are (perhaps *should* be) quite complex and require extensive time and effort. Others are simple and straightforward, requiring relatively minor amounts of time and effort.

The degree of complexity depends upon how one defines the "problem" to be solved by a particular curriculum. If the problem is defined by *the teacher or subject-matter specialist* and in terms of the learners' lacking skills and knowledge in a given subject matter, then the process is relatively simple: obtain a reputable text and set of readings or laboratory exercises, decipher the understandings and skills apparently envisaged by the author, and state these in an appropriate form.

However, if the matter is viewed more broadly, as a goal or goals derived from an analysis of *trends* in society and in the sciences and the humanities (which predict the nature and scope of "life problems" learners will be coping with in their futures), then the process of defining goals and objectives becomes more complex and demanding.

The first process is more practical (in one sense) and probably the procedure of choice for beginning system developers. The second is more ideal, especially if provisions are made for incorporating the thinking of a diverse representation of all a school's audiences. This ideal process (to be discussed more fully) yields the greatest assurance that the educational system is producing graduates who have the skills and understandings necessary to make a contribution to the suprasystem — society as a whole.

Regardless of how goals are initiated, it is obvious from Chapter 2 that goal setting is a critical first step. All future decisions and system-development activities flow from the goals established as a first step. The goals must, then, be *formulated* in ways which permit — and, to some degree, control — subsequent steps in system development.

THE FORM OF INSTRUCTIONAL GOALS

It is assumed here that the reader is either personally competent to decide the *content* of goals or is functioning within an institution that has the competency to determine the goals for all courses or learning experiences. The institutional competency may or may not include a procedure for involving learners themselves in the process of defining goals, but it is assumed that there exists a prior ability to decide what skills and understandings the educational institution is to be held accountable for achieving. It is beyond the scope of this book to resolve issues involved in curriculum development, such as, What skills and understandings are necessary, important, helpful, or just nice to know? or, Should there be separate and distinct curricula in history and the social sciences for students of diverse ethnic and cultural origins? These issues and many others will be left to educational theorists who have considered the alternatives and articulated their opinions more thoroughly than the present author.

The only observations the author will make about *content* may be summed up as follows: First, there is no unequivocal research evidence that one body of skills and understandings is *better* than another, at least in the sense that learners who have mastered any particular body of skills and understandings are more productive and happy than those who have mastered others. If there are indications of such effects, they are that individuals with *broad* competencies in solving problems are more useful members of society than those having narrow, exclusionary, competencies. Specialization is not denigrated in this view; it is seen as an outgrowth of prior development of a broad competency base.

The author's second observation is this: To achieve the goal of a broad competency base in learners, it will be necessary for educators to establish goals of "developing interest in" or some such reactive behavioral outcomes. Few educators presently accept responsibility for such "affective" outcomes! The tendency is to view "interests" and "preferences" as mystical components of personality. The concern of educators is, therefore, to determine what preferences preexist in learners and to cater to them rather than to provide experiences to *develop* interests.[1] In the writer's personal view, for example, all educational goals should incorporate an intention for learners to expect or anticipate satisfaction from engaging in activities similar to those in the learning experience. Only thereby will the educational institution succeed in producing graduates who possess the *diversity* of problem-solving skills required for effective participation in a democratic society.

Determinant of Form: Purpose

To turn from *content* of goals and objectives to *form*, one must first consider *why* goals and objectives are important, and what *function* they perform in the process of system development. The *form*, then, must conform to purpose.

System goals represent the contribution to be made by a system to the suprasystem. Goal statements, as used in instructional planning, must describe that contribution in all its attributes. If the goal is a form of linkage between a system and the suprasystem, then subgoals and objectives represent a linkage between subsystems and the system and are derived from an analysis of system goals.

In an educational or instructional system, the contribution to the next larger system consists of changes in learner behaviors. Learner responses are modified as a result of learning experiences. Educational goals, therefore, must be stated, for planning purposes, in terms of the *behaviors* that are to characterize the learner when he leaves the educational institution and enters the larger system.

Since goals and objectives provide a basis for selecting and sequencing learning experiences (the design of instructional processes), the statements must not only describe the terminal behavior, they must also describe the *conditions* under which it will be displayed. If it is desirable for learners to become adept at analyzing events in an actual meeting conducted under parliamentary procedure, rather than simply memorizing rules for conducting meetings, then the goal should specify that learning is to be demonstrated under the "live" conditions rather than by taking and passing a paper-and-pencil test. By thus specifying conditions, the instructional designer is forced to include experiences in a practice setting (perhaps simulated) rather than simply providing textbook exercises on parliamentary procedures. It is conceivable, even likely, that a text or workbook study experience *will* provide some of the verbal skills useful for analysis of real events and thus constitute a *portion* of instructional designs.[2]

A third purpose of the statement of goals and objectives is to provide a basis for formulating measures that provide feedback to both the student and the instructor. Feedback to the student provides reinforcement through confirmation of correct responses and serves as a cue for review or other additional study when responses are incorrect. For the instructor, feedback is an indicator (or cue) that instructional processes are or are not functioning as planned.

This third purpose, as explained previously, is partially served through including a description of the behavior and the conditions under which it is to be demonstrated. However, for statements of goals and objectives to be fully functional for the development of measurement processes, they must indicate *how well* the behavior is to be performed. This *terminal performance level* is a description of behavior that specifies such matters as: how fast, how accurately, for how long a period of time, the maximum number of errors permitted, and so forth.

A fourth purpose of statements of goals and objectives is to *communicate precisely* to learners and others (such as parents) just what capabilities are to be expected as outcomes of a sequence of learning experiences. To satisfy this requirement, statements of goals and objectives must be formulated in terms which describe observable conditions, events, and behaviors.

Consider, for example, the two following statements of educational objectives:

1. Students, upon completion of this unit, should be able to integrate the research from the three theories of intelligence into a common conceptual model.

2. Students, by the end of the unit, should be able to demonstrate, by submitting five reports of individual test administrations, that they are able to interpret intelligence test reports in terms of three different theories of intellectual functioning. Each of the five reports is to contain an indication of how identical test performances are interpreted differently by different theorists, to describe the probable future course of development of each subject as would be predicted by the different theories, and to include a statement which draws upon research from all three theories to produce a prediction of the future development of test subjects. The reports are to be judged in terms of the criteria and guidelines contained in the leaflet entitled "How to prepare a Psychological Report."

Obviously example (2) contains much more information for the learner. It *avoids* the use of ambiguous terms such as *integrate* and *conceptual*. It describes the skills and understandings that are to be demonstrated, in language that communicates a complex chain of behaviors. The statement even specifies *how well* the behaviors are to be manifested by referencing a criterion document. The student who is exposed to objective (1) is in a quandary as to what is expected of him. A future employer having a student's skills explained to him as in example (1) will still be unsure of just what abilities the student actually possesses. Objective (1) is an example of a "fuzzy" (ill-defined abstraction). It is imprecise. It communicates little except that in some way the learner is expected to "deal with" different theories and somehow bring them together.

The fifth purpose of statements of goals and objectives is to relate learnings to the life experiences of learners. This is particularly true of the broader goal statements, which provide the basis for the planning of total instructional systems. (Subgoals and specific objectives for the array of subsystems and individual learning experiences need only be related to goals.)

The purpose of establishing relevance to life experiences is probably best accomplished by including information as to the future *applications* of the cluster of skills and understandings to be developed within a defined block or *module* of an instructional program. This means, to use John Dewey's term,[3] that statements of educational goals should include a description of the *instrumental* character of learning—that is, the learnings should be useful in "problem-solving."

As an example, consider the following statement of a problem: All indications are that in the near future, you are going to be asked to vote or otherwise indicate your decision about the best course of action the government should take regarding pollution of streams, lakes, oceans, and ground water supplies. You will be faced with much confusing and conflicting evidence and with research studies that yield different answers. In other words, you will have to evaluate contending claims about (1) the sources of water pollution, (2) the best ways to prevent and clean it up, and (3) *who* should direct the whole effort. To evaluate the claims and reach your own decisions, you will need to be able to do the following: (1) define the technical terms in the field and (2) summarize existing research in water pollution.

Goals for instructional systems, which provide the learner with a description of the instrumental nature of the learning, should go far in providing a set for learning, and in directing learner attention to future cues or out-of-classroom cues that will encourage transfer or generalization of learning.

To briefly recapitulate, the subsystem for defining goals and objectives serves its purposes and makes its contribution to the total development process by producing statements which:

1. Describe what learners are to be able to do by:
   a. using verbs that denote observable behavior
   b. clearly specifying the stimulus that evokes behavior
   c. indicating the objects, persons, or events to which the learner responds
2. Describe the conditions (both physical and psychological) under which the behavior is to be demonstrated
3. Describe how well the performance is to be demonstrated
4. Use descriptive terms in common usage to communicate precise expectations of learner and avoid use of "fuzzies," or ill-defined abstractions.
5. Relate learning to problem-solving requirements faced by learners outside the classroom.

Specificity of Statements of Purpose

There exists among educators today an issue as to how "specific" one should be in describing instructional outcomes. The point is made that statements which describe behavior very explicitly are often trite and relate only to inconsequential learnings.[4] It is held that the more specifically outcomes are written, the larger the number of statements required and the greater the effort involved in preparing them, with possibly little gain.

No doubt, these are valid assessments of *many* statements of educational goals and objectives. The overall criticism is not valid, however. Statements of goals and objectives are prepared for definite purposes related to planning and design and to the process of learning. No statement of outcome is "too" trite or inconsequential if it aids either planning or learning. The judgment is made on the basis of functional utility, not the superficial topography of the statement.

Instructional systematizers must develop through experience the capability to determine just how specifically goals and objectives should be stated. Experience will indicate that learners of lower developmental levels are helped by more *explicit* statements while those of higher developmental levels are sufficiently cued by statements that only *imply* specific learnings.

There are, as yet, no well-validated rules for making such judgments. The author has frequently used the following nomenclature to *discuss* (not prescribe) the different levels of specificity:

1. Educational Goals — statements that describe broad problem-solving skills — and that can be broken down by analysis to obtain
2. Instructional Goals, which specify the skills necessary to solve "components" problems and can be further analyzed to yield
3. Instructional Objectives, which specify discrete chains or clusters of responses or skills and can be further analyzed to determine
4. Behavioral Objectives, which describe unitary responses under limited conditions

The above levels do not, of course, refer to concrete aspects or characteristics of a statement of purpose, and the classification scheme is thereby limited. Since no two planners will agree on the appropriate level for placement of all statements, its principal defense is *utility*. It can be used to guide a planner in the processes involved in establishing objectives.

Having described the *output* of the subsystem, which is functionally responsible for defining and establishing goals and objectives for the instructional system, it is time to consider the *processes* by which an instructional planner can actually prepare statements of goals and objectives for the instructional system under development.

SPECIFYING GOALS AND OBJECTIVES

It is a truism in all systems approaches that there is more than one method or process by which to produce an end product. Following this thought, it is the instructional system developer's task to select the *best* method or approach to define and establish instructional goals from among several alternative approaches. Before examining alternative approaches, perhaps it will be helpful to reconceptualize just what the product is to be. Fig. 3.1 has been prepared as a model to represent the product of the subsystem for defining and establishing instructional goals and objectives.

From Fig. 3.1 it is apparent that the product consists of a series of statements describing outcome learnings. The statements are generated successively through analytic processes so that as one moves

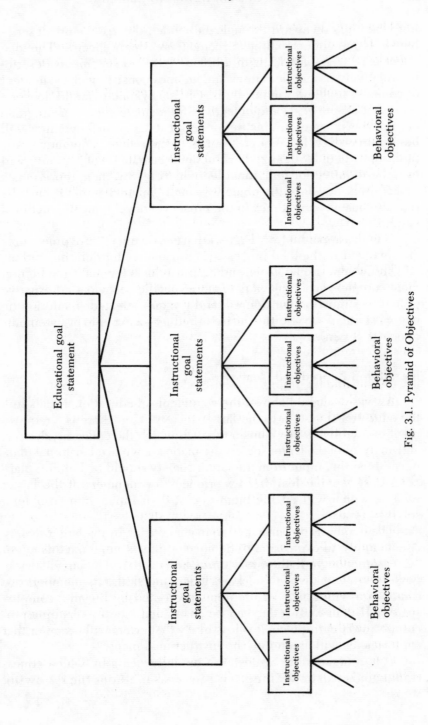

Fig. 3.1. Pyramid of Objectives

from the top downward through the model, the statements describing skills and understandings become increasingly specific. The total effect is of a "pyramid," with a broad "base" of statements describing relatively minute learnings and an apex consisting of a statement of complex problem-solving skills. Obviously, one pyramid does not represent all the goals and objectives for a single course or program, not to mention an entire institution. A great many such pyramids will be required even for a single course. If the school is operating on a philosophy of individualized instruction, separate set of pyramids will even be required for individual learners! Fig. 3.1, then, represents a process that develops the objectives for a "microsystem"; it must be repeated many, many times in the process of developing instructional systems.

It is also apparent from Fig. 3.1 that two distinct sets of procedures are involved in the total process: (1) procedures for defining and establishing educational goals, and (2) procedures for analyzing higher, more complex, goal behaviors to more specific behaviors. Alternative procedures must be considered, and the one selected should be the one most likely to yield the desired product—a pyramid of statements of objectives and goals.

Identifying Educational Goals

As was discussed above, the statements of educational goals link the educational system to the larger society. Thus there is a requirement to establish a mechanism through which the concerns, desires, and analyses of the larger society are made known to educational planners. Since this input from the larger society should be helpful, planners must provide learning experiences for members of the larger society, which will enable them to cast their inputs into "problem-solving" terms.

The emphasis on participation in goal setting by the larger society is not simply an expression of democratic ideals, although this might be reason enough. Rather, it is a *pragmatic* action. The larger society possesses a vast diversity of knowledge and skills. Its members are aware of a wide range of problems presented by life in a complex society. If their knowledge can be channeled into the planning process at a very early stage, it is less likely that errors will occur, or that irrelevancies will creep into the instructional plans.[5]

It is now possible to design a model process by which educational goals can be defined. This process includes the following steps:

1. Representatives of all recognized "audiences" of the educational institution are identified and recruited to participate and to speak for their constituencies. "Audiences" include (but are not limited to):
   a. parents
   b. students
   c. employers
   d. minority populations
   e. labor unions
   f. special-interest groups (environmentalists, political parties, religious bodies, etc.)
   g. public and private agencies (police, welfare, labor department, armed forces, news media, etc.)
   h. higher education — academic disciplines
   i. taxpayers not represented above
   j. professional groups (lawyers, doctors, accountants, artists, etc.)
   k. teachers and educators
   l. older population
2. Representatives of audiences meet in small groups for orientation to their tasks:
   a. purposes of goal setting in educational planning
   b. nature of educational goals
   c. overview of process
   d. information about major social-cultural trends that indicate problem-solving skills needed by learners in existing situation and in future
   e. Task groups are formed with representation from diverse audiences
3. Task groups meet to prepare reports (may include minority reports) on what problem-solving skills the educational institution should be held accountable for achieving.
4. Each task group elects a representative who presents the report to an assembly of representatives of all task groups.
5. Entire assembly elects a review committee to work with a team of specialists in reviewing reports produced by task groups: eliminating duplications, resolving conflicts, rephrasing statements to more clearly specify behavioral outcomes, noting "gaps" or inadequacies in final list, etc. The team of specialists assesses each entry to determine such matters as:
   a. Is the proposed outcome consistent with the law? (For example, does it violate the constitutional provisions regarding religion in the schools?)

    b. Is the proposed outcome consistent with what is presently known? (For example, are goals describing skills in self-care in the health area consistent with the findings of medical research?)

    c. Is the proposed outcome *feasible* within present and foreseen economic and physical constraints? (For example, is it feasible for the schools to provide vocational skills beyond what is required for *entry* into a vocation?)

6. Review committee submits the refined list of goal statements to assembly of representatives for discussion, clarification, and approval. Two or more approval cycles may be required to obtain final approval by assembly.

7. Finally, the approved list of goal statements is submitted to the legally authorized board for official adoption. The board review may result in referral back to the assembly, which may, in turn, require recycling back to any prior step and a repeat of the process.

This long, tedious process presents many problems, not the least of which is that of maintaining high levels of attention and effort by participants. An essential element of the process must be that of providing reinforcing feedback to all participants to maintain their involvement. Each step must be carefully planned, with objectives clearly stated and with attention given to multitudinous details. Skilled personnel must be obtained and rehearsed in their roles of expediting the group processes. All in all, it is an extremely involved, time-consuming process. It is justified, however, by the results: statements of educational purpose based on the widest variety of inputs from the total society and on an analysis of life requirements. It is reasonable to expect also that the larger society will more readily come to accept the value of a diversity of educational outcomes by reason of having participated in an activity like the one described here.

Alternates to the Social-Involvement Model

Several alternative approaches may be (and have been) used to formulate educational goals. Three will be described here, two very briefly and one in more detail because it is a somewhat more feasible process for individual teachers than the social-involvement model.

One process frequently employed by schools may be referred to as a "historical, intuitive-analysis" process. In this approach, the history of educational practices over the years and surveys of

present-day practices are studied to factor out the common and enduring purposes that appear to characterize education through the ages.
If one assumes that the enduring purposes persist because of some
intrinsic merit, then there might be reason to assume that such merit
will continue in the future: these assumptions are difficult to validate.

A second process might be termed the "paragon model." In this
approach, one first describes an idealized hypothetical person (the
"educated man," "Renaissance man," "scientist," "productive
worker," etc.). The characteristics of the "paragon" then describe the
"outcomes" of an educational program. This approach assumes first
of all that one *can* adequately describe such a person, and secondly
that such characteristics are valid for all times and all places. Both
are highly questionable assumptions, and certainly many groups in
the larger society would challenge any such singular formulation for
their children.

If the "historical-intuitive" and the "paragon" models rest on
dubious assumptive bases, what approach can be used by the individual teacher who wishes to systematically individualize instruction
and learning in his course? Obviously, he cannot, acting alone, implement the social-involvement model.

The best answer appears to be to reduce the social-involvement
model to manageable proportions and approximate it as closely as
possible.

To accomplish this, the individual teacher should probably begin by asking himself a series of questions:

•1. From my understanding of events in today's world, what appear to be the life problems my students are going to be required to solve in the next ten or twenty years?
2. What skills and understandings from my area of specialization
   will be useful or helpful in solving the above problems?
3. What skills and understandings will learners need to transfer
   from other disciplines or specialities or will have to be
   provided them as supplemental learnings in my course?
4. How many *optional* goals can I offer as choices to my students?

As the list envolves, the teacher, qua systems developer, will ac-
tively seek inputs from as broad and representative group of advisers
as possible (including present and future students). Most assuredly,
teachers or institutions that receive graduates of the course or program should be oriented to the goal-setting process and then asked to
evaluate the evolving list of goals. Their inputs into the process should

consist not only of their notions as to life-problem-solving skills, but also the *levels* of skills and understandings they expect their students to possess upon entry into their classes. It is legitimate to consider future educational-learning experiences as problems to be solved and to provide learners with appropriate preparatory experiences.

As overall goals are defined and expressed in terms of behavioral outcomes, the teacher can progress to the next step, that of analyzing complex behavioral descriptions to define the more specific goals and objectives.

GOAL-ANALYSIS PROCEDURES: A GENERAL SCHEME

Goal analysis requires the instructional-systems developer to have already mastered the "content" of his field. He must be knowledgeable about the component skills and understandings that combine to form the higher-level, problem-solving competencies.

However, this knowledge base alone is seldom sufficient for the process of goal analysis. Additional skills and understandings are required; skills in the use of an analytic method for identifying the different *kinds* of learnings and an understanding of how the different kinds relate to one another. Before detailing all the steps in the process, it is necessary to examine a conceptual scheme or model for analysis. The scheme is one which permits the planner to identify components of problem-solving skills in terms of a *hierarchy of learnings*. It derives largely from the work of Robert Gagné as described in his book *The Conditions of Learning.*[6]

Gagné has distinguished eight types of learning. They are arranged from the simplest, S-R (Stimulus-Response) conditioning type, up through steps of gradually increasing complexity to the highest level of problem-solving. Each type is related to observable behaviors and performances, which are the products of each class of learning. Only a brief overview of Gagné's hierarchy is possible here, and the reader is urged to obtain his book for a more complete review.

Since the concern here is with the *application* of Gagné's hierarchy in the analysis of goals, the sequence of presentation will be reversed from that found in Gagné's book. Rather than beginning with the simplest level (which Gagné refers to as "signal learning") and building upward, the sequence employed here begins with the complex behaviors and through successive analyses identifies the simpler component learnings.

Problem-Solving Learning

According to Gagné, the highest level of skill learning is problem-solving. This learning involves developing skill in the *use* of basic principles, concepts, and verbal skills to achieve one's goals. The application skill is, in effect, a type of higher-order principle learning, an approach or method. Traditionally, problem-solving skills are related to internal and nonobservable (therefore inferred) processes in our abilities to think, to reason, to behave rationally. Problem-solving behavior is based upon prior mastery of relevant *principles,* which are the first component learnings identified through the process of goal analysis.

Principle Learning

In this class are placed all learnings that we commonly refer to as scientific laws and theories, procedural rules, grammatical conventions, and so forth. Typically a principle declares some form of relationship between concepts: For example, "aggression by humans leads to either overt or covert counteraggression" states a relationship (causative) between the concepts of aggression and counteraggression. "If the noun is feminine, then the article *la* is required" states a conventional rule for selection of the form of the article in French. The knowledgeable teacher can readily identify the principles, rules, and conventions which are useful in solving problems in his field, noting each in the form of an objective. Each principle-learning objective then may be analyzed to define the *concept* learning; according to Gagné, this must precede the learning of principles.

Concept Learning

Concepts are often referred to as *abstractions,* words or terms that refer to characteristics or properties of objects or events and permit one to classify or categorize. Thus *red, square, precipitation, furniture, atoms, tape, ten, divide, multiple, democracy, dictatorship, perspective, north,* all represent concepts. Each term refers, not to a specific object or event, but to a set of *attributes* or characteristics. The term *table,* for example, refers to attributes of (1) a flat surface, (2) legs or other arrangement to support at some height, (3) some usefulness, (4) made from a limited (but growing) set of materials, and so forth. Wherever these characteristics are observed, the object is classed as a table, a member of a class of objects in which there exist several variations to the extent that actual resemblances may be rather slight.

In concept learning, we see the processes of generalization and discrimination. It is desirable for learners to generalize the term *table* to respond to all articles of furniture that are clearly tables. It is also desirable for them to discriminate between *tables* and *buffets*, which have characteristics common to tables but also distinguishing attributes. The learning that occurs in making such differentiated responses is an example of bringing behavior under the control of stimulus conditions — with the stimulus condition being that of abstract properties of objects and events.

After stating the concepts as learning objectives, it is possible to identify the many *discriminations* that must be made by learners before abstract concepts can be learned.

Multiple-Discrimination Learning

Learning of this type involves the learning of different responses for easily confused physical stimuli. In learning French, for example, one learns to distinguish *faim* ("hunger") from *femme* ("woman"). In becoming a mechanic, one learns to distinguish a carburetor from a fuel pump; in botany to identify as different organs the stamen and the pistil, in music a quarter-note from a half-note.

In preparing instructional objectives, the teacher will note discriminations that require specific attention and state them as proposed outcomes. From these statements it is possible to identify still more basic learnings, *verbal chains* or *verbal associations*.

Verbal-Association Learning

In its simplest form, this type of learning consists of developing the ability to *name* an object or event. Verbal equivalencies, such as are involved in the translation of a foreign language into English or changing a technical term to a term in more common usage, are other examples of this type of learning. In each case, the learner response is in actuality a *chain* of verbal responses.

In developing a set of instructional objectives, the teacher will note which verbal associations students are likely to need to learn in the course of mastering the concepts, etc., and will state these as objectives.

Unfortunately, at this point the analytic scheme begins to break down, in that the next three classes are not derived just from a consideration of the next higher class. These learnings are more in the realm of complex muscular skills and eye-hand coordinations or in the "affective," or emotional, realm. As such, they are often preconditions for learning the higher-order objectives described above, but they are not necessarily *identified* through an analysis of the learnings themselves.

Chaining

If one carefully examines *each* of the foregoing types of learning, it is often possible to discern a number of discrete physical actions which are linked into a standard sequence. For example, learning a foreign language involves mastery of a chain of lip, tongue, and jaw movements in concert with diaphragm and laryngeal muscles in the coordinated production of a particular sound. The new sound may be quite unlike any the student has learned previously. Also, if one examines the behaviors at the problem-solving level, it is obvious that various *tool skills* are often needed to apply various principles.

Identification of learning objectives of the class termed *chains* requires the systems developer to be able (and willing) to specify the kinds of physical activities that are involved at *all* other levels. Once these objectives are specified, it is possible to identify the smaller response units, which Gagné classes as *stimulus-response learnings*.

Stimulus-Response Learnings

Learning of this type consists of discrete movements of the skeletal system, the so-called psychomotor skills. These movements are learned as a function of reinforcement for successive approximations to the desired movement. Children learning cursive handwriting skills, for example, are successively reinforced for grasping a pencil correctly, holding it at the correct level, making vertical, horizontal, and circular movements, and then for combining these basic movements into coordinated chains. Reinforcement or feedback is provided for closer approximations on successive trials. The learning of complex skills in manipulating tools, even precision instruments, is simply a matter of learning separately each item in a series of discrete actions, then combining them into complex chains.

Signal Learning

Learning at this level involves acquiring a conditioned response to a specific *signal*, or cue. The responses are often diffuse and emotional in nature. Fear responses at times of threat (tests, requirements to speak before a group, etc.) are examples of inappropriate learning at this level. "Interests," "values," and so on, are examples of desirable outcomes.

This learning process is usually referred to as *classical,* or *respondent,* conditioning as described by Pavlov. Learning at this level is of concern to the teacher, because *prior* signal learning often interferes with higher-level learning, and the teachers must set highly individualized objectives for students. The "timid" child, the aggressive child, the child who is easily distractible, the child who cannot "concentrate," all probably represent learners whose prior conditioning experiences developed behavioral patterns that interfere with learning experiences. Although behavior-modification research has provided classroom teachers with reliable techniques for reversing the effects of such conditioning, the function of many teachers is only to identify the existence of individual patterns and then obtain specialized consultation from counselors, school psychologists, or social workers.

OTHER ANALYSES

The Gagné hierarchy is concerned mainly with cognitive learnings — that is, the development of the ability to deal symbolically and intellectually with objects and events. This is the traditional realm of the schools. School learnings have always emphasized the development of verbal skills. Certainly our society requires such skills, for it is a verbal society, and to survive and thrive in it, one must have verbal capabilities.

However, certain complex learnings are not so clearly verbal in nature, yet are equally important in solving life problems.[7] Teachers as designers of instructional systems must be able to analyze life requirements to identify these critical learnings.

One such set of learnings might be characterized as *stress tolerance.*[8] It is well recognized that individuals having cognitive skills often make erroneous decisions at times of stress or pressure. They impulsively make inappropriate statements (falsify, become sarcastic, use "humor" to lighten tension, etc.), or they impulsively attack others or flee from stressful conditions. From an analysis of the real world we know that all students are going to encounter stress conditions in which they are: (1) being evaluated by others, (2) required to meet deadlines or work under pressure of time, (3) required to perform with accuracy or precision, (4) required to make an unpopular decision, (5) required to endure some physical pain or discomfort, (6) engaged in some form of conflict, (7) required to explain a mistake or error.

A complete education will provide for the development of their abilities to tolerate these and other stresses. In other words, when under stress, they will continue to act in ways which achieve personal goals and objectives, rather than in impulsively avoidant or aggressive ways.

Closely allied to stress-tolerance objectives is a body of skills that may be referred to as *social skills*. These learnings, which often include as a component "ability to accommodate to stress," provide an individual with the skill to:

1. Join cooperatively with others for achievement of common goals
2. Respond to others in ways that reduce conflict and interpersonal stresses
3. Encourage and reinforce others
4. Provide others with clear communications about oneself
5. Act as a leader or manager of the activities of others
6. Instruct or train others
7. Evaluate the outcomes of the efforts of others
8. Ascertain the conditions under which other persons work and accommodate one's expectancies and demands to those conditions
9. Participate in a wide variety of enjoyable group activities
10. Assess one's own capabilities and make commitments to others which can be kept

These capabilities, as in the case of stress-tolerance abilities, are not readily identified through systematic task-analysis procedures. Objectives describing such outcomes will likely be formulated only from a careful analysis of the conditions that prevail in work, recreation, home and family, religious, and civic or organizational settings.[9]

A final note on stress tolerance and social-skill objectives: the perceptive reader has already noted that these objectives involve much of what is termed *attitudinal* learning. *Stress tolerance* and *social skills* are preferred terms inasmuch as they are more descriptive of *observable behavior* and refer less to an unobservable, inferential "inner state." Such behavioral categories tend to cue instructional planning better than do abstractions.

Many teachers will be concerned that, thus far, no recognition has been given to such outcomes as "appreciation of aesthetic or expressive experiences," "commitment to peace," "valuing of worth and dignity of others," "sensitivity to rights and feelings of other people," "recognition of man's oneness with all of nature," and "acceptance of differences among individuals, cultures, and ethnic groups."

In all likelihood, these and similar statements represent important educational outcomes. As stated, however, they are of little direct use in planning and so do not function well as objectives. System developers who wish to focus on these statements are urged to take such concepts as *appreciate, commitment, sensitivity, worth and dignity,* and reduce them to *behaviors,* which can be directly observed. Experience has shown, as reported by Mager,[10] that a behavioral analysis of some of the above terms will result in naught. They do not refer to anything observable. Some of these concepts, which we commonly use to describe behavior, are *evaluative,* not descriptive. Use of such terms is part of our own learned behavior and we use such terms as *appreciate* and *sensitivity* to communicate *approval* or *disapproval* of the behavior of others, not to *describe* it.

The preceding paragraph reflects a fundamental position with regard to educational outcomes. Educational planners should not include statements denoting motivational states as learning objectives. If such states do actually exist, they are not observable or measurable. We always "infer" a motive state from *behavior.* Why not simply begin by describing the behaviors and skills that will be useful to the individual? If he *behaves* in socially effective ways, his motives (attitudes, etc.) will be evaluated as "good" by most of his associates.

PROCEDURAL STEPS IN IDENTIFYING INSTRUCTIONAL OBJECTIVES

It is helpful for the beginning systems developer to use detailed cues to lead him through the complex chain of steps in preparing a complete set of instructional objectives. For this reason, prepared forms and worksheets are advocated. As one becomes more experienced, reliance on forms may be reduced.

The first step is to reproduce a supply of forms (mimeograph or lithograph). Multiple copies of the worksheets included as Figs. 3.2, 3.3, and 3.4 can be made rather inexpensively and will serve the purpose quite adequately. Note that different forms are required to cue or direct the cognitive analysis, the stress-tolerance analysis, and the

CURRICULUM PLANNING WORKSHEET
IDENTIFYING COGNITIVE-SKILL OBJECTIVES

Educational goal _____

Instructional goal _____

Page _____

Principle learnings	Concept learnings	Multiple-discrimination learnings	Verbal-association learnings	Psychomotor chains	Stimulus-response learnings

Fig. 3.2. Sample Worksheet for Identifying Cognitive Objectives

CURRICULUM PLANNING WORKSHEET
IDENTIFYING STRESS-TOLERANCE OBJECTIVES

Educational goal _____

Instructional goal _____

Page _____

Evaluation stresses	Time stresses	Accuracy requirements stress	Interpersonal conflict stresses	Explaining mistakes or errors	Physical discomfort	Miscellaneous sources of stress

Fig. 3.3. Sample Worksheet for Identifying Stress-Tolerance Objectives

CURRICULUM PLANNING WORKSHEET FOR
IDENTIFYING SOCIAL-SKILL OBJECTIVES

Educational goal _____

Instructional goal _____

Page _____

Cooperative-activity skills	Skills in encouraging others	Leader managerial skills	Evaluation skills	Adaptation to others' requirements	Self-assessment skills	Miscellaneous social skills

Fig. 3.4. Sample Worksheet for Identifying Social-Skill Objectives

social-skill analysis. Teachers wishing to develop instruction for goals in the areas of sensitivity, appreciation, and commitment will need to develop their own worksheets according to whatever analytic scheme they devise.

The second step is a listing of the problem-solving skills that have been identified as the educational goals for the instructional program. A separate planning cycle is required for each. The statements in this list should be designated by Roman numerals.

Next, each goal statement should be written in summary form in the appropriate space in the upper-left-hand corner and the Roman numeral in the space designated "Page" on each of the three worksheets.

Next, prepare a statement describing the *cognitive* skills that are seen as components of the problem-solving ability and summarize this for entry in the space labeled "Instructional Goal" in the upper-right-hand corner. Follow the same procedure to describe the stress-tolerance and social skills that are component behaviors. Add capital letters *A*, *B*, *C*, to the page designation for cognitive, stress-tolerance, and social skills respectively. Within each of the three instructional goals, the pages should be numbered consecutively by Arabic numerals. For example, pages I-A-1, I-A-2, and I-A-3 represent the first three pages of cognitive learning objectives for goal (I). Pages enumerated III-C-1, III-C-2, and III-C-3, represent the first three pages of social-skill learning objectives for goal (III). It is advisable to maintain this or a similarly elaborate indexing system. There will be many occasions during the system-development process for referring back to these initial worksheets.

The entries in the columns on the three worksheets do not constitute complete statements. At this point it is concerned only with *describing behaviors*. Thus, under "Principle Learnings" one might indicate:

1. Able to predict consequences of continual disposal of nitrogenous wastes into lake and streams
2. Able to describe effects of minor keys on listeners
3. Able to predict the effects of increased altitude on the boiling point of water
4. Able to predict and describe the effects of using too great temperatures in welding of aluminum parts
5. Able to describe effects of cessation of reinforcement

Each of the above objectives refers to established principles — but specifies an *application* of the principle *as a behavior*. Number (1), for example, relates to the abstract principle that as the amounts of nitrates and nitrites in water increase, there are correlated increases in the aqueous plant population and a consequent decrease in available oxygen for support of aquatic animal life, leading to eutrophication of bodies of water. Number (4) relates to principles that specify the boiling point of aluminum, the temperature at which oxidation occurs very rapidly and at which aluminum crystalizes after cooling. Note that in each underlying principle, there are two or more concepts and a relationship is specified between the concepts. In number (1) "increased amounts of nitrates and nitrites," "increased aqueous plant population," and "decreased aquatic animal life" are all concepts. The relationship is that increases in one lead to decreases in another — a cause-effect relationship.

In the column headed "Concept Learning" such learnings as the following should be entered: (1) able to define *nitrate* and *nitrite*, (2) able to define *aqueous plant population,* (3) able to define *aquatic animal life,* and (4) able to define *correlated.* These again state the objective in terms of learner behaviors.

Subsequent steps involve following the scheme derived from the Gagné hierarchy. Teacher judgment is required to estimate how far down the hierarchy he and his students will require the analysis to proceed.

Another judgment must be made also in this analytic process. Often it will be found, when analyzing principles to identify concepts, that subordinate principles are involved. For instance, in the above example it may not be sufficient simply to define *nitrate* and *nitrite* to achieve the principle-learning objective. There must first be principle learnings that involve understanding the dependence of plant growth-rates on supplies of available nitrogen. The teacher must make these determinations as he proceeds, estimating the effects of not specifying such learnings, and, if the effects would limit achievement of the objective, inserting the subordinate principle as a learning objective.

As a significant point, it should be mentioned here that the systems developer will find it necessary to work back and forth across the columns, making the best estimates he can as to the need for additional learning objectives.

ESTABLISHING COMPETENCY LEVEL OR TERMINAL-PERFORMANCE CRITERIA

In the preceding examples, the behavioral outcomes were indicated or described. The next step involves specification of *how well* the behavior is to be displayed and under what *conditions*.[11] To aid in this process a form similar to the one shown in Fig. 3.5 is suggested; it can also be inexpensively reproduced.

As a start, copy each behavioral or learning outcome entered in the various columns on the three previous worksheets in the space labeled "Behavior." Also, indicate the page reference in the appropriate space in the frame.

For each behavior, a *judgment* must be made as to the *nature of the product*. To elicit this decision, the systems developer should ask himself, What can the learner *produce* within the time constraints and the limits of other resources that will best demonstrate he has developed the defined ability?

Obviously, correct answers to paper-and-pencil tests are a "product" that demonstrates ability. However, this is only one way to demonstrate abilities, and not at all the best in many instances. Moreover, true-false, multiple-choice, short-answer, or other so-called objective tests are not the only or the best form of paper-and-pencil tests. These limited methods of demonstrating competence tend to measure short-term recall and learnings, which are so cue-specific that only limited transfer will occur for many learners.

If a paper-and-pencil test is used, it is suggested that items require learners to:

1. Describe real-life applications of a principle. For example:
   a. Briefly describe the chain of events that you predict will happen in the water of the Red River when and if the sewage-treatment plants in three population centers break down.
   b. How will most beginning piano students react if they are asked to first learn "Three Blind Mice" in a major key, then transpose to a minor key?
   c. If a standard cookbook recommends boiling dried beans for three hours, what change would be necessary if you lived at an elevation of five thousand feet or more?
2. Write examples of concepts. For example:
   a. Describe the events that occur as the boiling point of a metal is approached and exceeded.
   b. List five examples of naturally occurring nitrates and nitrites found in the surface waters of this region.
   c. Describe three correlated pairs of events you have noticed.
   d. Examine the three sets of diagrams provided below; each of the five diagrams in each set represents some aspect of plant

CURRICULUM PLANNING WORKSHEET
SPECIFICATION OF TERMINAL-PERFORMANCE LEVELS
AND CONDITIONS OF MEASUREMENT

Behavior: (＿＿＿＿＿)	Performance level:
Conditions:	
Behavior: (＿＿＿＿＿)	Performance level:
Conditions:	
Behavior: (＿＿＿＿＿)	Performance level:
Conditions:	

Fig. 3.5. Sample Form for Specifying All Elements of Complete Objective

growth under different conditions of nitrogen fertility. Prepare a chart illustrating the relationship in each set and then briefly describe the degree of correlation.

3. Correctly identify and label parts of actual pictures or diagrams for multiple-discrimination or verbal-association learnings. For example:

a. The following diagram shows an electric fuse box with numbered arrows pointing to the various parts. In the numbered spaces below write in the name of the parts indicated by the numbered arrows. Identify with circles the parts that should not be touched in the process of changing a fuse.

b. In the following picture there are four types of clouds. Circle and label each. Place an asterisk by the cloud type which usually precedes a weather front.

The above examples of paper-and-pencil-test items require learners to generate their own answers and to consider cues other than just words. Answering them involves more mental activity than simple recall. Therefore, we have some reason to think that the learnings they represent will be retained and will transfer.

Retention and transfer, however, can be expedited by learning to produce products other than written descriptions. Actual projects can be assigned in which principles are applied and data collected. A videotape or film of an event (a group meeting in session, a plant growing, a cell dividing) can be shown and learners required to analyze the event, predict what will happen next, or explain what has just happened. Vocational students can demonstrate their skill by disassembling and reassembling simulated machines or equipment.

The point is, the systems developer should take the initial specification of behavior and convert it to a "test" condition. The test condition is then described in the objective.

Next, a decision must be made as to how well the learner should perform on the test. The systems developer should ask himself such questions as:

1. How many test questions should be answered correctly?
2. How fast should a project be completed?
3. How many errors are permissible?
4. What qualities of response should be looked for?

The answers to these questions should be entered on the second form as per the examples provided below:

1. Behavior: Able to predict consequences of continued disposal of nitrogenous wastes into lakes and streams.

   Condition: In a test—using three sets of diagrams of differing sizes of mature plants under differing conditions of fertility.

   Performance level: Student able to produce three accurate charts illustrating correlation and to write a statement estimating the degree of correlation between rate of growth and fertility.

2. Behavior: Able to predict and describe the effects of using too great temperatures in welding of aluminum parts.

   Condition: Provided a sample of welding in which two strips of aluminum have been joined.

   Performance level: The student will be able to identify three of four points at which welding temperatures were too high and orally describe the effects on adjoining metal and predict effects at these points when weld is stressed.

From the entries made in this worksheet, the systems planner may then proceed to stating his objectives in their final, most communicative form. The two examples may be synthesized as follows:

1. Students will develop the ability to predict what occurs when nitrogenous wastes are constantly disposed into lakes and streams. This ability is indicated by developing three charts which accurately show what happens to plant growth-rates when the level of nitrogen from waste is increased. The charts are to be made from diagrams of plants and plant products and are to be accompanied by a written estimate of the degree of correlation between plant growth and the amount of nitrogen.
2. Students will know what happens to welds when the welding temperature gets too high. This ability is developed by learning to point out to the teacher where, on a sample of actual welding, the temperature was too high and to explain to him what the effects were on the nearby metal and what will happen to the weld at these points when it is placed in use.

These rephrasings have been prepared for younger or less experienced students. The phrasing and vocabulary level would likely be modified and the statement shortened for older or more verbal students. The systems developer's post-experience with learners is the best guide to phrasing and vocabulary level.

RECAPITULATION

It has been shown in this chapter that the subsystem for developing goals and objectives for an instructional system must produce statements which: (1) are useful in planning and (2) communicate to learners just what is expected of them. These purposes are best met by statements which: (1) describe the actual behavior students will display after learning has taken place, (2) the terminal-performance level, and (3) the conditions under which the behavior is to be displayed.

It was suggested that procedure used by the systems developer to identify educational goals should involve many other people or "audiences" of education and that goals be stated in the form of descriptions of abilities required for solving life problems.

Once goals have been stated, an analytic scheme, such as one based on Gagné's hierarchy of learning, is recommended to identify more specific behavioral outcomes in the cognitive learning areas. Other types of specific objectives in stress-tolerance and social-skill learning areas were identified through an analysis of life conditions faced by students *outside* the classroom. A series of figures illustrated forms suitable for cueing the systems developer through the analytic process.

ADDITIONAL AIDS IN PREPARING INSTRUCTIONAL OBJECTIVES

The procedures advocated in this chapter for specifying objectives represent only one approach of many that are possible. Also, the discussion of the Gagné hierarchy is, of necessity, very brief. It represents only one of several possible conceptual schemes for organizing what is known about learning.

It is recommended that readers, before attempting to follow the procedures described in the preceding pages, become thoroughly familiar with the works cited in the notes and the list of suggested readings for this chapter. Some of the writers mentioned present analytic schemes that differ from the one described in this chapter. The differences need not confuse the reader. Simply consider them as alternatives and judge which is more useful from the viewpoint of your individuality.

CHAPTER 4

Preparation of Self-Instructional Materials

PROBLEM: USING CRITERIA TO SELECT FROM ALTERNATIVE MODELS

Having specified the outcomes of the instructional system and having established how well learners are to perform the behaviors, it is now time to design the component *processes* of the instructional system.[1]

Experienced teachers know that there is always more than one way to achieve instructional objectives. Some instructional processes are better than others for achieving some kinds of learning, while other outcomes seem to be products of other methods and approaches.

It is fundamental to the systems approach to include procedures for comparing alternative instructional processes and selecting the best of those available. Since the emphasis is on developing a program for individualized instruction, the subsystem for design of instructional procedures must produce a design which: (1) permits learners to progress at their own rate, (2) permits and encourages learners to exercise options as to the skills and understandings they will develop, (3) provides learners with the skills to design and develop their own learning experiences, and (4) specifies a teacher function compatible with individualized learning.

Also, since the instructional process must conform to overall constraints imposed by society and by the institution, the procedures in a particular course or program should: (5) provide gains in skill and understanding, with least cost per unit-gain, (6) function within the framework of schedules established by the institution, and (7) be compatible with what most students and patrons consider to be, or are willing to accept as, *learning* experiences.

In addition, from what is known about the learning process itself, the instructional procedures should: (8) require minimum amounts of learner effort for each unit of gain, (9) provide frequent reinforcing feedback during the process of learning, (10) provide learners with sufficient opportunity for *practice* under conditions of feedback, (11) permit students to demonstrate that *prior* learnings have given them all the skills and understandings required for *entry* into the learning experience, and (12) provide experiences in combining simpler, more basic skills and understandings into complex abilities and in generalizing learnings to other settings.

And finally, since schools function within a democracy, with certain governing ethical considerations, the instructional processes must be adaptable to individuals having different and varied backgrounds, including prior limitations or enrichments in verbal experiences, exposure to cultural expectations, and development of different patterns of secondary reinforcements (values, interests, attitudes).

The above characteristics of a "good" instructional process constitute a set of gross *criteria* for selecting and designing instructional systems.[2] Using the criteria as guides, it is possible to select from among several alternative instructional procedures, despite the fact that each procedure may achieve defined objectives.

The total task of producing instructional materials that accomplish the above purposes breaks down into two subtasks: (1) *design* of instructional system and (2) *production* of materials.

The preceding subtask designations (or sub-subsystems, if one retains a conceptualization of the entire curriculum-development process as a system) suggest that it is first necessary to develop a "blueprint" for instruction; next one follows the "blueprint to construct the system.

DESIGN OF INSTRUCTIONAL SYSTEM

There are two routes one may follow in designing an instructional system. The first leads to the selection of an overall design or *model* from among those currently described in professional literature or available commercially. The second involves creating or inventing a design to fit the particular set of objectives and constraints that characterize a program and institution. The purpose of both routes is the same: to make a prior decision that will lead to improved decisions at later points in the development of materials.[3]

Selecting from Available Models

There are good reasons for adopting a model which has already undergone development and testing. One is spared much labor, many of the "bugs" that inevitably emerge in a new program are eliminated, and there are usually a number of "how-to" references or consultants available to solve problems of materials development. Many of the process models have been developed into complete instructional "packages" with reading and audiovisual materials, workbooks, and laboratory or experience guides available, and with correlated tests and other feedback devices ready for use. Such packages are available from publishers and other suppliers who often make results of evaluation studies available, so that there is a basis for forecasting the effectiveness of the materials.

Despite the advantages, it is not always possible to adopt a ready-made process model in toto. The particular circumstances of a given program will usually force instructional-systems developers to modify ready-prepared materials to a greater or lesser degree. Commercially available packaged programs particularly require modification. They typically achieve objectives different from those derived from an analysis of problems. Quite often they are geared for learners with ability levels different from those in a given program. They frequently require teachers to function in ways for which they have not been prepared. A common practice is to utilize *parts* of packages, rather than packages in their entirety. The teacher as a systems developer thus retains greater control over the outcomes of instruction.

In passing, it should be noted that it will be appropriate, in many areas of learning, to adopt an entire package. In basic skill areas (reading, mathematics, spelling, etc.) this would be the case, since the objectives are similar for practically all learners in all institutions. In vocational-technical areas, where technicians are prepared for careers, the packages (such as prepared courses in computer programming, electronics, etc.) may be quite appropriate for any school or training program.

For most educational and instructional goals, however, it will be necessary for the teacher to select and develop his own materials for individualized instruction. He will need to work from a model or blueprint which he has evaluated and modified for his unique situation.

Evaluating Alternative Models

Space limitations do not permit an evaluation of all possible models or even a description of them. The list of suggested readings for this chapter contains several references that will introduce readers to details of various models. The various models may be typified as:

1. Contracting models, in which learners enter into agreements with the instructor to achieve objectives in exchange for rewards
2. Individually prescribed instruction models (IPI), in which all aspects of instruction are mediated by materials or by one or another of the emerging technologies, such as computer-assisted instruction (CAI) or printed directions for study, as in Individually Guided Instruction (IGI)
3. Discovery models, in which learners are exposed to basic experiences and data and required to evolve and formulate their own concepts and principles to solve problems in which they are interested
4. Interaction models, in which learners develop conceptual and other verbal competencies as a function of verbal interactions in small groups, which are stimulated by provocative questions and discussion leads

The systems designer should examine each model in terms of how well it satisfies the criteria listed in the opening section of this chapter. It is reasonable to assume that all of the models, *if properly implemented,* will be effective in achieving most objectives, but that some are more effective than others for achieving some types of objectives. The systems developer, then, must determine how much modification of the basic model is necessary to accommodate to the objectives he has identified. If a particular plan requires extensive revision or modification, this is probably reason enough to disregard it.

Evaluating the Contracting Model: An Example of Applying the Criteria

The contracting model offers an excellent example to illustrate how criteria may be used in making instructional decisions. The contracting model (usually referred to as "contingency contracting") was originated by Lloyd Homme and is described in his book *How to Use Contingency Contracting in the Classroom.*[4]

In contingency contracting, the learner agrees to follow a series of steps to achieve a selected cluster of objectives. Pretests are administered to determine whether the learner (1) has the necessary entry abilities and/or (2) has already achieved the objectives and is therefore "ready" to move directly to the next set of learning experiences.

The contracting model requires instructors to contract with the student to provide rewards and reinforcers (contingencies) when students demonstrate they have mastered the competencies specified by the objectives. Often, multiple-feedback procedures are used to indicate to learners that they are making small-step progressions toward agreed-upon competency levels. Recognizing from experience and research that individuals respond to different rewards, Homme prescribes a reinforcement "menu" and allows learners to select their own reinforcers. Typical reinforcing menus will include a variety of reinforcing events (RE) such as: (1) a specified number of minutes visiting with friends, (2) time out of class to spend in student lounge, (3) time to play cards or checker game, (4) opportunity to listen to a taped broadcast of a recent football game, (5) opportunity to read a magazine or book of choice, and (6) writing personal letters, etc.

In the contracting model, learners typically begin by contracting to complete teacher-designated materials and activities to achieve the teacher's objectives. Gradually, throughout the program, the amount of teacher-imposed structure is systematically decreased and learners are offered options to design more and more of their own contracts, to the extent that they eventually perform even the initial analysis for identification of objectives. In other words, Homme intends for learners to become "self-contractors"; in this role they presumably obtain practice and reinforcement for managing their own learning or for becoming their own "teacher."

Complete and detailed records of learner progress are maintained to provide teachers with: (1) an overall assessment of how the system is "working" and (2) "diagnostic" data on the progress of individual students.

The contracting process is very much a "teacher-materials" instructional system. As such, it is an analog of the man-machine system discussed briefly in Chapter 2. The plans for the system, then, must prescribe functions and objectives for the teacher as well as for materials.

To what degree does this process meet the criteria for a "good" model for individualized instruction? To aid in determining the answer, the criteria are converted to questions, and answers are derived from the description of the model.

1. Does the process permit individuals to progress at their own rate? Obviously it does, since the teacher contracts with each student individually, and the student works on his own to complete the

contract. It is even possible to contract with a small group that is undertaking a project. In turn, each individual member then contracts with the group to assume partial, but defined, responsibilities for the project.

2. Does the process permit and encourage the student's exercise of choice? Yes, although not at first. Students gradually learn to assume more responsibility for making decisions and planning their own curriculum.

3. Does the process provide learners with skills in the design and development of their own learning experiences? Yes, if it is properly implemented, most students will develop such abilities gradually over the course of a period of time.

4. Does the process clearly specify the role, responsibility, and function of the teacher? Yes, or rather it *requires* the teacher as a planner to decide what objectives he is to be responsible for achieving.

5. Does the process permit the use of low-cost techniques and methods? No technique or method is excluded by the model – so long as it yields gains in learner competencies. The systems developer is free to select any method or technique available. The overall model allows the teacher to make "trade-offs," that is, to substitute less efficient (but less costly) methods, and still achieve objectives where cost considerations are critical. If learner time is the dominant constraint, more costly techniques may be incorporated (if cost factors are less crucial).

6. Does the process operate well in all scheduling arrangements? Yes, students can start and stop at almost any point. Modular scheduling arrangements, however, seem to be tailormade for the contracting process.

7. Is the model compatible with what most people consider to be education? Not 100 percent, since some people consider an activity "educational" only when students sit in rows, listen to a lecture, then take a test. The contracting process and its rationale, however, can be described and explained satisfactorily to most parents and patrons. Some will view the reinforcement process as a form of "bribery," so special efforts will have to be devoted to providing them with a research-based rationale for this aspect of the process.

8. Does the process require a minimum amount of learner effort per unit of gain? Certainly not automatically. The model does, however, permit selection of materials and learning experiences that make learning very efficient. This is an important consideration since there is reason to believe that rapid, easy learning facilitates retention and transfer.

9. Does the model provide for frequent reinforcing feedback to learners? Yes, it has been developed specifically to provide such feedback.

10. Does the model provide learners with opportunities to practice recent learnings under conditions of feedback? Yes. Where it is necessary for learners to repeat learned activities for practice, the materials can be designed to provide for such exercises.

11. Does the model provide learners with opportunities to demonstrate their mastery of all objectives. Yes. Tangible reinforcements and rewards (contingencies) are given on the basis of demonstrated competency. Tests, projects, and direct student demonstrations of skills are all possible within the contracting model for displaying competencies.

12. Does the model provide experiences in combining simpler, more basic skills and understandings into more complex skills and understandings? Nothing in the model requires that learning experiences deal with simple or complex outcomes. The model permits both the use of materials which break learnings down into extremely small steps, and the combination of small-step learnings into more complex skills, if the abilities of the learner impose this requirement.

13. Is use of the model consistent with our democratic ideals? It would seem so, although there is no consensus as to just what the term democratic ideals includes. By use of carefully constructed materials, learning experiences can be provided all students, regardless of ethnic background (characterized by differing values, family structures, etc.) and differing "interests." The process is tailormade for students from cultures that eschew competition and "winning over the other guy," since contracts are highly individualized. It is also tailormade for instructional situations where there are a number of learners who have had very restricted or very enriched backgrounds. Materials can be prepared for learners of any entry skill level.

From this assessment, the contingency contracting model appears to be ideally suited for adoption as a general process plan for the individualized instruction system. There are some "weaknesses," however. Teachers will likely need to carefully orient parents and patrons to the model. The model alone does not guarantee outcomes. There still remains the problem of developing materials to fit and support the model.

It is possible, of course, that the other models will satisfy the criteria equally well. The reader, to qualify as a systems developer, will want to go through similar evaluation processes with one or more of the models presently available. The answers to the assessment questions should then be compared as a basis for making a final decision. If two or more "score" the same, then the teacher is in the enviable position of being able to exercise a personal preference!

Constructing a Model

Although there are a number of advantages in selecting a model from among those already designed, there are circumstances which require the systems developer to design his own. Vocational-skill training programs (such as Manpower, Job Corps, or special programs for the handicapped, as examples) may be so conceived that available models do not allow objectives to be met, or institutional constraints may make the models inoperable.

Constructing a satisfactory model is no simple task. It requires high levels of competence in learning and instructional theory and research. Most classroom teachers, if required to design an overall model, will typically piece together bits and fragments of other models, frequently with no idea of how well the bits and fragments complement each other.

One process, however, will enable the neophyte systems developer to construct a unique process model or overall instructional plan to solve the problems posed by many situations. This involves conceptualizing the entire instructional process as a *simulation* of reality. In other words, the teaching-learning process involves the learner in an interaction with a *representation* of the real world in which he will later be required to use his newly developed competencies. The representation, or simulation, must provide the learner with exposure to many of the cues to which he will later be required to respond, to models and instructions on appropriate responses to those cues, and to reinforcers and rewards for making the modeled responses. The reinforcers and rewards must approximate those he will later receive in the real world, although they may not be equal in magnitude and they will probably occur more frequently and for smaller response units than in real life.

One example from the author's personal experience will serve to illustrate the potentiality inherent in the use of a simulation model constructed for a unique educational setting: a men's Job Corps center.

As the reader will recall, the Job Corps was established by federal legislation as a part of the War on Poverty. The purpose of the Job Corps was to prepare young persons from economically restricted backgrounds for "breaking out" of a life of poverty and entering into a productive, satisfying, and remunerative life. In problem-solving terms, the young people were to be provided with skills necessary for coping with the problems of making a living and contributing to the larger society.

From this overall goal, the next step was to ascertain the need of the young people for new and different coping skills. From sociological and psychological research it was determined that the prospective Job Corps members had marked deficiencies (compared to the levels required for successful employment and social participation) in:

1. Basic tool skills
2. Verbal skills (reading, writing, arithmetic, more abstract conceptual abilities)
3. Impulse control under conditions of stress
4. Social skills for dealing with authority figures, members of "higher" socioeconomic groups, conflict situations, and institutional bureaucracies
5. Self-esteem, as reflected in remarks refering to "hope for the future," or when making comparisons of self with others
6. Setting their own goals, then regulating their behavior to achieve their goals

From an analysis of these "needs" it was possible to establish a wide variety of specific behavioral objectives to be achieved by all Job Corps members.

An examination of the needs suggests that any instructional process that was heavily dependent upon verbal procedures would be likely to fail. Verbal learnings would occur, but the amount of transfer would likely be small. From the low levels of impulse control which characterized the learners, it was possible to forecast that obtaining and maintaining learner set would be difficult. A learning environment that was too "rich" would prove to be highly distracting. Finally, it was reasoned that unless some provision was made for developing and maintaining new social behaviors within the residential and recreational aspects of the young men's lives, social behaviors would not change. This was so because the young men would be interacting mainly with peers who held expectancies of each other (that is, provided cues and models) that were similar to those of their "home" culture, thus tending to reinforce the same responses that were originally produced by the home culture.

These special circumstances indicated that a unique training model was required, one which would enable the systems developers to incorporate a wide range of specific learning experiences for obtaining a variety of outcomes.

The decision was made early to develop a design that would *simulate* the "social reality" into which the young men would be moving upon completion of their Job Corps experience. This social reality was conceptualized as a "meritocracy," a form of social structure characterized by openness and upward mobility and in which reward or reinforcement is provided for individual productivity.

To carry out the meritocratic "theme," tool-skill learnings and verbal learnings were arranged to occur in long sequences with divisions being established at points which approximated those found in industry. For example, in the automotive mechanics training program, the entire training line was divided into the following job levels: (1) filling station attendant, (2) filling station mechanic, (3) quality check-out mechanic, (4) brake repairman, (5) front-end repairman, (6) power-train repairman, (7) carburization specialist, (8) ignition and electrical-system repairman, and (9) auto air-conditioning specialist.

By the time a corpsman had completed all the skills involved in "removing and replacing" parts in each of the above sections, using the tools that are designed for such purposes, he had the entry tool skills needed to perform satisfactorily at a beginning level in most garages. However, other skills were needed—verbal, impulse-control, and social skills. These skills and response tendencies were aligned along the training line to occur as much as possible at points where actual employment would require their use.

Within each training line, the actual learning occurred at "tool stations," which were enclosed areas (to reduce distracting stimuli) containing actual parts of an automobile plus relevant tools. Before going to the tool station, the corpsmen attended a "back-up" experience, which provided related verbal learnings (concepts, principles, etc.). Although the corpsmen worked in groups at the back-up sessions and the tool stations, progress was an individual matter. The tool stations and related back-up stations were designed to require a full day by the average learner, but faster learners moved more rapidly and slower learners found it necessary to repeat occasional stations.

The training line, which introduced corpsmen to all aspects of their chosen career in small steps, with massive feedback of success at frequent intervals, might be termed a *career simulator*. To achieve the broader social and personal development for life in a "meritocracy," it was necessary to plan all other aspects of the total program with equal care.

The residential program was thus utilized as a basis for many learning experiences. The living quarters were organized into four levels. As corpsmen progressed through career training, they were rewarded with "promotions" within the residential program. The first, or entry, level dormitories were rather plain and austere—comfortable, but certainly not elaborate. As one progressed up the "social-status ladder"—that is, as one received "promotions"—successive dormitory levels introduced noticeably more comfort, more privacy, more elegance of surroundings, and so forth. The level-four dormitory featured furnishings, recreational opportunities, and freedom to come and go comparable to those enjoyed by successful mechanics, construction workers, and restaurant chefs. The corpsmen, who could be "promoted" *only* on the basis of demonstrated learning on the training lines, were experiencing a simulated meritocracy, a social order in which rewards occur as a function of actual production, not simply for effort or for regular attendance.

It was recognized early in the program that even with the above-described simulations, many valuable social learnings would not transfer or generalize to the real-life setting. Consequently, within the residential program there were included additional simulation activities of a type known as *sociodramas.* Sociodramas are short dramatizations (carefully scripted beforehand) portraying the *consequences* of ineffectual social skills. Through guided discussions following the sociodramas, the corpsmen developed an alternative model for social behaviors that would lead to improved consequences.

For example, many corpsmen possessed limited skills in responding to authority figures (teachers, employers, policemen, etc.). Their responses, especially in conflict situations, tended to be highly aggressive or evasive and very frequently served to increase conflict, to engender a poor opinion of themselves by others, or to lead to other unpleasant consequences. After completing several related simulated experiences in which the consequences of alternative responses were clearly demonstrated, it was possible to see substantial changes in the behavior of corpsmen in conflict situations. They gave many verbal indications that they had developed a new set of "rules" for governing their social interactions with authority figures.

The foregoing example illustrates one way in which decisions at early levels in system planning influence and control decisions at later stages. Obviously, planners *could* have elected to use "uplifting lectures," peer pressures, or threats as processes for modifying social behavior. However, the decision to simulate reality as much as possible led to use of the sociodrama. The sociodramas provided a means to display the significant cues that should mediate behavior (and by careful design of the scripts, reduced distracting cues). The scripts could be as simple or as complex as necessary for learning to occur—something that is not always possible when lectures, peer pressures in group discussions, or threats of punishment are used to modify social behaviors.

A more complete description of the Job Corps program and its rationale has been provided by Woolman.[5] The reader is urged to study his article carefully to understand the broad significance of the simulation model for educational planning.

The discussion of alternative models has omitted the "logical" model, which is probably the model most commonly employed in education. Every subject field has, over the years, evolved a kind of internal "logic" which controls curricular decisions. For example, in mathematics, addition is learned before subtraction, multiplication precedes division. In biology one studies simple one-celled organisms before studying multicellular organisms. In history one follows a combined chronological-geographical progression.

This traditional academic model does not lend itself well to education for problem-solving, however. No model is acceptable for problem-solving education if it prescribes a sequence that the learner regards as arbitrary and unrelated to his purposes and goals.

This model does lend itself well to systematic treatment, however. The systems planner need only find a "good" text, identify some correlated readings and exercises—and many curriculum decisions are ready-made!

Also not mentioned is the "spiral" model, which conceptualizes a system or program as an ascending spiral with successive levels. The first spiral or phase introduces several themes or topics at a very elementary level. Successive spirals or levels expand each theme or topic to increasingly complex levels, frequently integrating themes or topics to develop application or synthesizing abilities. In many instances the spiral arrangement is simply a variation of the traditional academic model. It does assure a simple-to-complex sequence and does provide an opportunity for integration to occur. It may, however, suffer from the same limitations as the academic model. It usually is based on an analysis of knowledge in a field, not on an understanding of the purposes of learners or on a problem analysis.

Using the Model

Once an overall model has been selected from the alternatives, it is possible to move to some crucial steps in system building. To varying degrees, these steps are controlled by the decision to select one model as opposed to the others. The diagram appearing as Fig. 4.1 illustrates the decision-making steps.

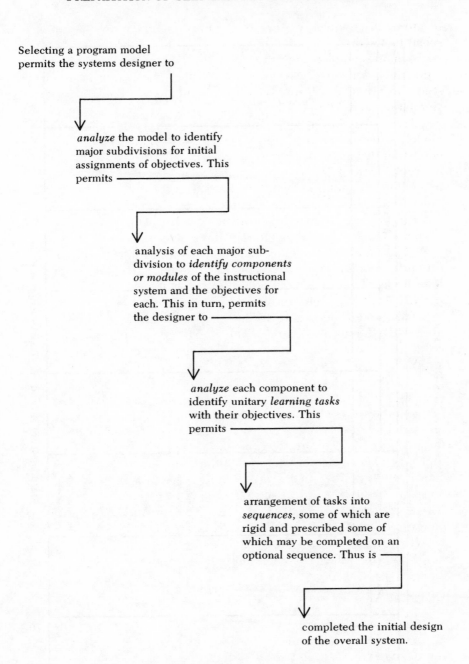

Selecting a program model
permits the systems designer to

analyze the model to identify
major subdivisions for initial
assignments of objectives. This
permits

analysis of each major sub-
division to *identify components
or modules* of the instructional
system and the objectives for
each. This in turn, permits
the designer to

analyze each component to
identify unitary *learning tasks*
with their objectives. This
permits

arrangement of tasks into
sequences, some of which are
rigid and prescribed some of
which may be completed on an
optional sequence. Thus is

completed the initial design
of the overall system.

Fig. 4.1. Steps in Decision-making Process
to Complete Design of Instructional System

LEARNING-TASK DESCRIPTION FORM

Task No. _____ Task title _____

1. Task description and objectives	2. Additional descriptors	3. Instructional elements	Component Analysis					
			4. Written-oral narration	5. Mediational technologies	6. Teacher mediation	7. Social-group mediation	8. Laboratory field experiences
		1. Orientation					
		2. Statements of objectives					
		3. Prerequisites					
		4. Pretest					
		5. Study guide					
		6. Learning experiences					
		7. Practice					
		8. Feedback 1. 2. 3. 4.					
		9. Evaluation					
		10. Succeeding activities					

Fig. 4.2. Model of Learning-Task Description Form

From the diagram it is obvious the goal of this initial process is to identify the individual learning tasks (with objectives specified for each) that make up the instructional system. Identification will always include a tentative title for the task and some *description* of the skills and understandings to be developed by the learning experiences within the tasks. A separate form should be initiated for each task as per the example illustrated in Fig. 4.2. Note that the learning-task description form includes spaces for more information than has been developed to this point. Entries for columns (2) through (7) will be developed in the next section. Also note that the example is much too small for actual use. The writer has found that legal-size paper is usually adequate, although even that size forces him to use many shorthand abbreviations for entries.

Returning to Fig. 4.1 to pursue the separate steps in the process of following a model to develop the initial system design, note that the first step is to analyze the model to identify the major subdivisions of the instructional system. If the model is a simulation model, the major subdivisions are likely to be ready-made. If, for example, a social studies teacher is planning to provide students with skills in understanding and participating in the decision-making processes of groups (such as committees, councils, legislatures, etc.) and has elected to simulate "normal" or "typical" development, the following major divisions may be identified from observations of the "natural" course of development:

1. Observer: reporter with skills in discerning major features of formal group processes, rules of procedure, and roles of various participants, and having the ability to describe these events
2. Petitioner: requiring skills in making presentations to a formal group, answering questions, representing others before a council, legislative committee, and so forth
3. Group member: needed skills are in debate and argumentation, in following more frequently used rules of parliamentary procedure, and in application of procedural rules to achieve own objectives
4. Group secretary: requiring skills in preparing minutes and other documents which summarize or make official records of group actions
5. Parliamentarian: having skills in using rules of procedure to resolve issues and to validate decisions and plans of group
6. Group leader: requiring skills in planning meetings, chairing meetings, summarizing issues, judging appropriateness of members' behavior, and so forth

7. Analyst/Evaluator: with skills in reducing complex procedural problems to basic elements, proposing new or modified rules for consideration, and relating procedures to historical and philosophical contexts.

The hypothetical social studies teacher has succeeded in identifying and describing seven subsystems, each of which can be further analyzed down to the level of an instructional task.

If the contracting model is adopted, it imposes no particular scheme for identifying major divisions. If it is used in the context of problem-solving education the same goal as above might be subdivided as below:

1. How does one describe the things which happen in a formal meeting of a council or legislature?
2. How can an outsider best influence the decisions of a formal group?
3. How can one best function as a group member?
4. How can one summarize and report on the actions of a group?
5. What are the procedures to follow in making decisions about the procedures being followed by a group?
6. What procedures and skills are needed to lead a group to make decisions?
7. How does one evaluate the functioning of a group?

This does not differ very much from the previous analysis. However, it tends to be somewhat more "academic" or even "textbookish" in tone, while the previous analysis yielded divisions which have a distinct flavor of "training" or "application."

Probably the reason for the similarity is the fact that both analyses were performed by the same person. Another systems designer would have derived two different sets of statements, with validity equal to those above. In all likelihood, the "problem-solving" analysis will yield major subdivisions compatible with objectives derived from the initial goal analysis described in Chapter 3.

The major subdivisions are next subjected to an analysis to identify component learnings. A component often represents a cluster of skills or understandings which possess a number of elements in which there is something common. Or, a component may represent a definable task with a product or outcome.

As a cluster of skills or understandings having a number of elements with some commonality, consider some modules derived from an analysis of item (4), "summarizing and reporting," in the second list:

1. Purposes of minutes and records
2. Contents of minutes and records
3. Form of minutes and records
4. Listening for preparation of minutes and records
5. Summarizing for clarity and conciseness
6. Preparing minutes and records to accurately indicate issues and controversies
7. Evaluating minutes and records

A little thought about each of the above will identify the commonality within each cluster of skills and understandings.

The second notion of a component is perhaps exemplified by the following statements from the same division.

1. Produce a statement that describes the job of a secretary, the skills required, and the purpose of his position.
2. Produce a set of rules that would govern the secretary in deciding what events within a meeting should be recorded.
3. Examine a variety of minutes and records of actual meetings, develop a format for minutes and records, and devise a system for maintaining official records.
4. Produce a set of notes from a videotaped session of the city council — check against audio-recording of session.
5. Prepare an actual set of minutes and records from notes.
6. Prepare a set of guides to follow in writing objective reports of group actions on controversial issues and decisions, etc.

Obviously, again, the differences are slight.

An examination of both sets of statements indicates that some are much more complex than others. It is possible that some could be reasonably completed by a student in a single setting; others are more complex and require much more learner time and effort. The division into learning tasks does not involve a process of analysis but a matter of estimating the appropriate task size. As a general rule, one would aim for tasks that require no more than one class session, plus outside activities, as a means to provide frequent feedback of accomplishment.

There will be instances where it is necessary to violate this rule of thumb. If some tasks are much longer, the sequence of tasks should be organized to place longer tasks after a number of shorter tasks. If at all practical, initial tasks should be very short, as many as two or three tasks per class session is not too many.

Perhaps it will be useful to the reader to have as examples some possible tasks identified from the previously described modules.

MODULE	TASKS
1. Prepare a statement of the duties of a secretary of a council or committee.	a. Study process of preparing a job description.
	b. Hear taped model of an interview, then conduct interview of secretary of a local group.
	c. Read an article on the job of a committee secretary and prepare a statement of duties.
2. Produce a guide for a secretary to follow in preparing reports.	a. Study Chapter 4 from "How to conduct a Meeting"; answer study questions on "Important things to note about meetings"
	b. Prepare a guide and obtain evaluations of at least two fellow students. Revise on basis of comment.

Obviously each of the modules could have been treated as a single learning task *or* as two or more tasks. The decision is arbitrary to a degree and is based upon the experience of the designer. The writer recently had the experience of designing a program for a one-semester beginning class in educational psychology. From the initial analytic process, eighteen tasks were identified. The first semester's experience with the program produced data indicating that almost a week was required to complete the average task, and that the students were expressing dismay at the "length" of the assignments. The following semester, the same content was divided among twenty-four tasks with the early tasks requiring only one day and the final two tasks requiring two weeks each. The data from this semester indicated that the total time required to complete all tasks decreased substantially and that concomitantly the complaints decreased markedly. The change in task size was not the only modification, but the experience did seem to confirm the wisdom of altering task size.

As each learning task is described in column (1) of Fig. 4.2, the specific behaviors that constitute the objectives for the task should be entered in the same column. These should be obtained from the original analysis, and as each is included on the learning-task description form, a mark or other indicator should be placed by the objective on the original list. This facilitates a check when all tasks are complete to make certain all objectives are included.

At this point, the writer usually completes column (2) on the form. This step is indicated because it frequently happens that the system model or a subsequent analysis suggests or requires additional objectives. For example, the contracting model specifies that learners gradually develop the ability to "self-contract," to manage their own learning. To develop this ability requires more objectives.

The writer has followed the practice of planning four phases for the development of these self-contracting abilities. For convenience they are labeled as —

Phase 1: Teacher-planned contracts. Essentially a habituation phase to introduce learner to content of contract and process of agreeing.

Phase 2: Teacher planned, but student shares responsibility for segments of contract — usually designs the process to evaluate performance.

Phase 3: Teacher instigated, student planned. Teacher defines problem and objectives. Student plans learning processes and evaluation.

Phase 4: Student controlled. Learner does all problem identification, setting of objectives, and planning of learning experiences. Teacher *prompts* planning, consults, and approves student planning.

In most programs at the public school and undergraduate levels, one only proceeds as far as phase (3). Phase (4)-type contracting tends to be used for independent study or self-directed study undertaken as a means for learners to delve more deeply into a subject or problem area than is permitted in a particular course.

PRODUCTION OF MATERIALS: A PROCESS MODEL

Before proceeding to the actual production of materials, it is necessary to draw up specifications for each task. It is usually helpful to decide first of all on a *process model*, which defines the elements of each learning task.

Elements of a Process Model

Space limitations do not permit a review of various models for the design of learning tasks. Instead, one model, which incorporates practically all the elements present in other models, will be presented and described.

The model assumes that the learner can understand language (either written or oral) and has a near normal complement of sensory and physical capabilities. If such is not the case, if the learners are handicapped in some fashion, it will be necessary to modify the model to accommodate to the learners' handicaps.

The model further assumes that the learning situation is such that learning tasks can be provided individual students in the form of *packets* or arranged in the form of *learning stations*. The model will specify the arrangement of elements for either packets or learning stations.

Also basic to the design of the model is a set of assumptions about learning. These may be paraphrased as:

1. Learners acquire skills and understandings best when they can predict ahead of time what they will learn during a learning experience.
2. Learners will perform more efficiently if they are provided guides to follow in organizing their study.
3. Learners will respond more positively where relatively short learning experiences are systematically reinforced.
4. Learners will learn more efficiently if materials and experiences are arranged into small steps.
5. Learners will retain learnings if there are adequate opportunities for practice of new learnings; transfer of learning will more likely occur if practice is afforded in situations approximating those for which transfer is appropriate.
6. Learners will integrate small-step learnings into complex skills and understandings if provided an opportunity in context of an evaluation activity.

The model prescribes that, for each learning task, students progress through the following steps, with each step representing an *element* of the model.[6]

1. Orientation. General objective — to provide student with ability to *predict* what and how he will be learning in the task, and to describe the usefulness of the skills and understandings and how they relate to previous learnings.
2. Statements of Objectives. General objective — to provide student with clear descriptions of skills and understandings, to

aid in planning of his work. Permits him to estimate what skills and understandings he has and to concentrate on the others.

3. Statements of Prerequisites. General objective—to provide students with assistance in planning, to determine whether study prior to undertaking task is necessary. This is especially important if tasks are arranged in rigid sequence.

4. Pretest. General objectives—to provide learners with confirmation of self-estimates made in steps (1), (2), and (3), and to allow students to demonstrate that prior learnings have resulted in mastery of skills and understandings included in the task objectives.

5. Study Guide. General objective—to provide learners with study questions, procedures, locations of materials, etc., which facilitate learner movements through the task.

6. Learning Experiences. General objective—to provide *input* to learner from readings, demonstrations, experiments, mediational techniques, laboratory experiments, etc., that will enable him to master objectives.

7. Practice. General objective—to provide learner with opportunities to rehearse new learnings, to increase speed and precision of response, and to learn to transfer responses to different settings.

8. Feedback. General objective—to provide learners with objective information as to how well they are mastering objectives or where more practice is necessary. This element should be repeated frequently during learning tasks.

9. Evaluation. General objective—to provide learners with an activity that requires them to integrate learnings and to provide them with feedback.

10. Succeeding Activities. General objective—to provide learners with preliminary information about the next step, the options they have (if any), and a general description of the next task or its alternatives. This element may also be employed to establish *closure* for a task.

The literature relating to details of alternative procedures for achieving the objectives for each element is extensive, too much so to adequately summarize here. Instead, the reader is referred to the list of suggested readings for this chapter. The following section, which describes the process of component analysis, will assist in clarifying the matter of processes to be used in achieving the objectives for each element within the process model. However, the reader is urged to study the literature before undertaking a systems development project. Then, as the system is developed, consult the literature again for solutions to specific problems as they arise.

Component Analysis

The reader has probably recognized that the objectives for each element of the process model may be achieved by several different methods. The purpose of the component analysis is to identify the method most likely to achieve the objectives for each element.[7]

The initial step in a component analysis is to identify the instructional processes available to the teacher. In the learning-task description form depicted in Fig. 4.2 and discussed in the preceding section, columns (4) through (8) indicate five general instructional processes or methods available to most teachers for mediation of learning (local circumstances vary, so teachers may need to modify this aspect of the task description form):

1. Narrative materials—both written and oral (as in a cassette tape-recorder)
2. Mediational "technologies," including:
   a. programmed texts
   b. teaching machines
   c. computers
   d. projectors and films
   e. television instruction
   f. charts-graphs-diagrams, still pictures, etc.
   g. simulation devices
3. Teacher mediation
4. Social-group mediation, including:
   a. role playing
   b. educational games
   c. discussion
   d. peer tutoring
   e. decision groups (committees, etc.)
   f. project groups
5. Laboratory/field experiences, including:
   a. structured laboratory experiments
   b. naturalistic observations
   c. conducted tours
   d. participation in science fairs

e. participation in festivals where art, music, and dramatic capabilities are evaluated

The second step is to identify successively, for each element of the model, the nature of the content that would be necessary for each potential method to achieve objectives of the task element.

For example, consider the various components under the "orientation" element in a task to develop "skills in preparing minutes and other reports of formal meetings."

Under the column "Written-Oral Narration" one might note: "two or three paragraphs explaining what is to be learned and how," and "audiotape segment giving explanation."

Under "Mediational Technologies" might be found "use first five minutes of film *How to take minutes.*"

Under "Teacher Mediation," "present oral explanation—two to six minutes."

Under "Social-group Mediation" could be entered "directed discussion with questions."

The column headed "Laboratory/Field Experiences" would likely be left blank in this example.

Step (3) involves estimating the probable weighting to be given each component somewhat as follows:

1. Estimate the *time* required of students to complete the materials described in the column.
2. Estimate the monetary *cost* of providing the materials under each component—such as five cents per pupil for rental of film; two cents per pupil for preparation—printing and distribution of narrative materials.
3. Estimate the development time required; such as, thirty minutes to prepare discussion guides.

Assuming that all instructional methods will achieve the designated objectives, the decision as to which among the four process components is a matter of selecting the "best" under the circumstances. Ideally one would select the method which requires the least learner time. However, if an "efficient" component exceeds cost limits or requires an exorbitant amount of developmental time, a process component of less efficiency would be accepted. This process is known as "making trade-offs," the deliberate sacrificing of one quality in order to assure another.

If there were a general rule to follow in making such decisions, it would be something like this: "Since individualized instruction requires many of the instructional inputs to come from materials, the "teacher-mediated" component should be used only when it presents a clear superiority on all three estimates over all other components. Thus, a systematic effort is made to reserve teacher time and efforts for the more significant activities described in Chapter 5.

After one proceeds through the component analysis for each element of the model and for each task, *specifications* for the instructional system are complete and it is time to begin producing the actual packets or learning stations.

PRODUCING LEARNING MATERIALS

The actual production of packets follows the specifications laid down on the learning-task description form (Fig. 4.2). The entries under "Component Analysis" specify the type and nature of the materials. The model element specifies the order, and the objectives determine the content.

In actuality, of course, the components analysis may specify that already developed materials be used. If a suitable film is available, the only development tasks are: selecting the portion to be viewed and preparing the study guide to help students locate and view the film and to view it with purposefulness.

This book is not planned as a text on instructional technique. The literature on research and experience with various techniques is extensive and cannot be summarized in the limited space available. The reader is encouraged, however, to review the works listed in the suggested readings for this chapter. In the following sections we will be content to deal with a few general rules for materials development that are especially applicable to programs of individualized instruction.

Preparing Narrative Materials

Written materials and audio presentations should be carefully outlined before being written. If the narrative refers to charts, tables, or pictures, such visuals should be indicated in the outline and the points to be drawn from each should be carefully defined.

Narrative materials should always be preceded by an exercise to make reading or listening purposeful (see below) rather than passive. The materials should be organized so that an active response is frequently required and feedback immediately provided. The frequency of responding should be higher for younger learners than for older ones. Primary students should be required to make an active response every minute or so, high school students no less frequently than one every five minutes.

The language should be appropriate for the age and grade-level of the learner. As new terms are introduced, they should be defined and examples provided. Every new term should be used as a basis for an active response with feedback.

Making Reading/Listening Purposeful

If a section of reading or audio materials is provided as an element of a packet, it should be preceded with a study guide that makes the reading or listening purposeful. Posing a few questions, and asking the student to read or listen for the answers, will usually accomplish this. If a psychomotor learning is to be achieved from a set of narrative instructions, it is often useful to precede the narrative experience with a (silent) visual demonstration and a suggestion that the actions demonstrated are to be learned from a reading or listening to the tape.

It is occasionally useful to employ a story or "play" to make reading or listening purposeful. For example, a short videotaped skit showing what can happen when safety rules are violated will tend to make reading or listening to those rules rather attentive.

Providing for Active Responding and Feedback

Most of the learning experiences in a packet or learning station should be of the "small-bit" variety with an active response being included as a part of each bit. The active response may be answering a question, completing a graph or chart, labeling a picture, producing an object or a piece of music, or writing an essay from a set of procedures or directions. Within seconds the student should be shown how near his response is to the criterion response and what to do if his response is inappropriate.

Development of Visual Materials

Insofar as possible, each learner should be provided with copies of graphs, charts, pictorials, or similar items that are needed for mastering objectives. This is in opposition to preparing an enlarged visual which is referred to by all learners. Do not use pictorials where it is feasible to use actual objects. This latter rule does not hold if the actual object is highly complex (such as a microscope). To instruct about complex objectives, use a series of line drawings, starting with gross features to be differentiated, and progressing through successive levels of detail as the series progresses. Clear plastic overlays can be useful in this task, although the writer has found no advantage over a series of line drawings.

Visual aids, such as films, videotapes, and simulation devices, should be provided students in *autotutorial* areas designed for one to four learners. These areas, commonly referred to as "carrels," should provide isolation from other learners and be equipped with all the mechanical and electronic devices, such as teaching machines, video-cassette players, and so forth, that are necessary for use of mediated materials found in the program. As learners are required to use the mediational materials, they move to the autotutorial carrels from a supervised or group-study area. Their packets contain instructions for operation of the equipment and direct them to the appropriate film, cassette, or slides.

The packet materials must also, as a rule, guide the active responses students are required to make to materials. All film viewing should be preceded by narrative inputs that raise questions or issues to which the film provides answers or clarification. Film viewing should always be followed by feedback for appropriate responses to the questions.

The preparation and selection of visual teaching aids is an extensive subject, much too extensive to treat here in detail. The reader is encouraged to consult the references on the topic included in the list of suggested readings for this chapter.

Technologically Mediated Instruction

The visual instructional aids discussed in the preceding section may be considered technological mediational devices. However, there is utility in considering them separately from a number of more complicated devices, many of which are electronic in nature and utilize more of the principles of learning in their functioning.

These automated devices are all descendants of the original teaching machines and programmed texts devised by B. F. Skinner and his associates. They employ various means of displays, all the way from a video tube actuated by a computer to a simple strip of paper moving past a slot or opening in a boxlike contraption. Some even have typewriters which ask questions or direct reading assignments; after the student has typed in an answer or a summary of a paragraph, the typewriter congratulates him for a correct answer or suggests a bit more thought or a rereading if the answer was erroneous!

Since the more elaborate, computer-assisted, equipment is not likely to be available to the typical school, it will not be considered here. The interested reader is referred to the appropriate references in the list of suggested readings.

However, many technological mediation processes are available to the teacher.

Teaching machines and programmed texts are available for use at all grade-levels in a wide variety of subjects. In an individualized instructional program they can be extremely efficient and effective for: (1) rapid development of concepts and principles, and (2) remediation of basic skill deficits. Typically, programmed learning exercises (either texts or teaching machines) should be of relatively short duration — say thirty minutes at the most. The high rate of reinforcing feedback tends rapidly to satiate many learners and they become bored. Programmed materials function best where the new skills are placed into use rather quickly. When they are included in the individualized packet, they should be preceded by a description of how they will be used and followed by a short application exercise.

Example: (Before the learner completes a short program on mathematical manipulation of decimals) "The next exercise to complete is a short review of decimals. When you complete the programmed text and the exercises, you will be able to solve problems that involve dividing tax income among the various agencies and programs in the state government and to prepare graphs and charts for showing the divisions." Immediately after the programmed study, the learner moves directly to the application experience.

Integrated equipment-materials packages are available in reading improvement, mathematics, electronics, and some other fields. Typically, the equipment is rather expensive and is limited to very few sets of materials. It is probably the course of wisdom to forgo the use of such package programs, favoring, instead, the purchase of basic equipment such as projectors, videotape players, and other equipment for which a wide range of "software" is available and for which teachers and schools can produce their own programs.

Mediational devices are improving, although many still require expensive maintenance. The essential problem is that they have not, as a general rule, proven to be more effective than a considerably less expensive combination of textual (narrative) materials, programmed materials, audio presentations, and visuals.

The question frequently arises, Should teachers prepare their own programmed materials for learning packets? No all-inclusive answer is possible. A great deal of time and effort are required to prepare and validate a programmed unit. Used appropriately, such materials will aid many learners. However, in view of the other demands on their time, teachers should not normally devote very extensive time to preparing programmed textual materials. It is better, it seems to the writer, to select programs available from commercial sources, then cut and fit them to the learning tasks.

There is one possible exception, however. It is often worthwhile to prepare very short "adjunct" programs for review or restudy purposes. A student, for example, who has read or listened to a narrative presentation and has failed to learn from it, can frequently master the objectives from a brief program prepared over the same content. Such programs need not be as meticulously prepared or use so many small-step frames. Consequently, time and energy requirements are relatively minor compared to the preparation of a program for original learning. There is still the question, however, whether the time and energy might not be better spent in making the narrative presentation more effective.

Social-Group Learning Experiences

Some kinds of learning seem to require group interaction. Abilities to discuss issues, engage in cooperative ventures, assume particular social-role functions, and tolerate social stresses simply do not develop for most individuals from verbal experiences alone.

The problem for individualized instruction is obvious. How can one plan or design a group experience that will provide sequenced experiences for individuals? Difficulties in answering this question have led many to reject the basic idea of individualized instruction. This is true especially among teachers who see the social learnings as being of paramount importance.

The writer sees three possible ways in which learning experiences can be designed to achieve social-skill outcomes.

First, include directions in selected packets on how to function as an instructional assistant; then, on a rotational basis, assign students to a tutorial function within the program, thus enabling them to learn skills involved in helping others.

Second, develop a number of packets as "project learning" experiences in which groups of students follow a guided procedure to (1) analyze the learning task, (2) divide the project into individual responsibilities, (3) collaborate on a final product, and assume different responsibilities for such functions as leading the group, assembling resource materials, coordinating activities, and evaluating group operations, thus learning skills in cooperative activities.

Third, develop a number of sociodramas in which social responses are modeled within a brief play or skit. The first element of the script should portray the details of a social situation (with only relevant cues). The situation should represent a problem that one participant in the drama is obviously inept in solving. The script should clearly indicate the *consequences* of his ineptness: he fails to achieve his goal. After the skit is presented to an audience of five to eight members, the entire group analyzes the elements of the skit by responding in discussion to a set of questions about the portrayed events, such as:

1. What was (name of inept character) trying to do (what was his goal)?
2. How was he going about it?
3. How did (the other character or characters) react?
4. Why did he (they) react that way?
5. What did (name of inept character) do when he (they) acted that way?
6. Did he achieve his goal?

These questions are followed by a summary emphasizing a vocabulary different from the one used by participants in the analysis-discussion, a vocabulary using less "emotional" words and "explaining" the sequence in terms of behavioral principles.

The next step involves a set of leading questions to elicit suggestions from the group for *alternative* responses that *could* have been made to the problem situation by the inept character. For this purpose the entire scripted episode is divided into defined parts which reflect "critical incidents." For each incident the leader asks: "What would have happened, do you think, if (name of inept character) had tried (such and such an alternative behavior)?" Then, after discussion, the leader asks for other alternative responses to be suggested by the group members.

After the alternatives are all described the leader says: "OK, (name of inept character) could have acted differently—what would have happened if he had? How would the other person have behaved?" Following this discussion the group formulates a general rule to follow in social situations of the type portrayed by the drama.

In all three methods, note that the social learning experiences are *structured*. As students learn to perform in the structured experiences, the amount of imposed structure can be reduced and the students can design their own structure and test it out. The task materials can be phased over an entire program to permit gradual *fading* of structure and increased assumption of planning responsibilities by learners, even to the point of the students identifying needs for specific social skills.

Laboratory-Observational and Field Experiences

Several kinds of learning objectives require students to manipulate materials, visit out-of-school sites, or make observations of naturally occurring events. Packet materials should include materials which provide procedures to be followed by the students as they progress through the process.

For such experiences, narrative procedures should be accompanied by a *demonstration* or *model* of procedures. In sequence, the materials should:

1. Present a demonstration of the action *without* verbalization on the basis of simple instructions to view the demonstration or film.
2. Repeat the demonstration with verbal description.
3. Have the student verbalize the action as he views it.
4. Have the student actually carry out the action.
5. Provide the student with feedback on his performance.
6. Arrange for repeat if performance is below criterion levels — start repeat at step (2).

For laboratory experiments or crafts-type activities, special workspace, equipment, and supplies must be available, and the procedures for setting up equipment and obtaining supplies must be included in students' materials.

Evaluation of Student Performance

In addition to the feedback materials provided students, it is necessary to prepare materials for final "check-out" exercises on each packet and for each module. To prepare these materials the teacher should:

1. Refer back to original objectives to determine (a) terminal-performance levels and (b) conditions under which behavior is to be demonstrated.

2. Examine packet design to determine if (a) and (b) are still feasible within constraints of design.
3. Decide to either retain (a) and (b) or rewrite them to conform to assessment of packet—still keeping in mind the overall objective or goal, and making the new criterion performance-levels and conditions appropriate.

It is likely that many of the evaluation activities will consist of traditional paper-and-pencil tests, and this is probably appropriate. However, many, if not most, teachers will need to greatly update their test-constructing abilities to adequately measure progress through individualized learning experiences. Otherwise, tests will tend to require rather simple "recall" by students. It is strongly recommended that teachers develop the ability to devise tests which measure comprehension, analysis, synthesis, and evaluation type abilities. A careful study of *The Taxonomy of Educational Objectives: Cognitive Domain* by Bloom and his associates (see list of suggested readings for this chapter) will help teachers develop the ability to prepare tests for these higher-level abilities. A careful study of a small book by Dorothy Adkins Wood, *Test Construction,* will give directions on preparing different types of items and on procedures for planning a test (see list of suggested readings for Chapter 3).

Not all learning tasks are evaluated by tests, however. Project reports, demonstrations of psychomotor ability, actual production of materials (such as scale drawings, maps, simple circuits, or mechanisms), and oral presentations of results of research or study are all more appropriate than paper-and-pencil tests for some kinds of objectives.

Where tests are used, they are usually not provided students as part of task materials but are simply described. The nontest evaluation materials are frequently included. Where evaluation activities do not consist of a test, packet materials should describe the activity fully and explain the performance criterion precisely. This will tend to reduce error and will lead students to accurate decisions as to their readiness to "check out" of the packet or module. The descriptive materials on all evaluation activities should inform the student of his options if he fails to achieve criterion performance levels.

RECAPITULATION

The preparation of instructional materials from objectives involves two broad planning steps: (1) overall design of a program—deciding upon a "model"; and (2) preparation of materials.

The overall design or model may be selected from previously developed ones or may be developed by the teacher. In any event, the selection process involves applying *criteria* of goodness, not just selecting on the basis of personal preference.

Once an overall design or model has been specified, the program can be successively subdivided through modules, tasks, and units to identify the smaller bits of learning experiences.

Each bit, or learning task, can be divided into elements, with each element having its *process objectives*. From a component analysis the "best" method can be selected for each element according to cost, time, and feasibility considerations.

Various rules of thumb are provided to guide the actual development of materials, but the reader is urged to review the extensive literature on instructional methods and materials before actually preparing the materials.

CHAPTER 5

Implementing the Instructional System

In the preceding chapters the emphasis was on the development of materials for guiding *students'* behaviors. In this chapter the emphasis turns to the development of guides for *instructors'* behaviors.

Earlier, an instructional system was likened to a man-machine system in which a worker and a machine perform complementary functions to produce a product. In education and training, the term should probably be *man-materials system* (or *person-materials system*, to avoid sexist overtones). In either case, the point is that preplanning of the behavior of instructors must be carried out as carefully and thoroughly as the development of the self-instructional materials.

No doubt, the amount of *control* over teacher behavior implicit in the above statement will provoke resentment on the part of some readers. However, it must stand. Instructors have, with the best of intentions, subverted well-designed instructional programs. Well-conducted instructional activities have, on the other hand, rescued poor materials. Careful planning of the actions of teachers can reduce subversion and increase the effectiveness of materials.

Careful planning of instructor functions serves a purpose in addition to that of enhancing student learning. It permits an accurate evaluation of the developed system.

Actually, of course, an instructional system is never "developed" in the sense that it is completely finished. Objectives change, new techniques are invented with the promise of greater efficiencies, and the membership of student groups changes from time to time. These constant changes mean that instructional systems must constantly be adapted, always be in a state of development.

Each implementation of an instructional system constitutes an experiment, a test of how well it functions as a whole to achieve goals and objectives and of the effectiveness of each part. The component

91

of the system referred to as "instructor" or "teacher" is likely to be the most influential or significant aspect of the program. The functions of this aspect, in interaction with the functions of other aspects (materials, the physical environment, etc.), must be as carefully planned as the interactions of other aspects.

Otherwise, the activities of teachers will vary in unpredicted ways, as described previously, and there will be no sensible way to evaluate the functioning of the system or its components. If functioning cannot be assessed, there is no way to rationally modify the system.

Evaluation of system function requires that accurate and extensive data be collected by the teacher. Historically, the impressions and opinions of teachers and students have been used as data on which to base decisions about instructional effectiveness. Experience, however, has revealed that such data are usually unreliable and are so ambiguous as to be of only limited use for planning purposes.

Implementation of an instructional system, then, requires the teacher to organize and plan his activities to: (1) enhance the effectiveness of materials for developing learner skills and understandings, and (2) systematically collect evidence of system effectiveness. The planning strategies for accomplishing these two purposes are considered in the two following sections.

SYSTEM IMPLEMENTATION I: MANAGEMENT FOR LEARNING

In Chapter 4 it was recommended that when an instructor is planning the elements of learning tasks, his direct responsibilities should be held to a minimum. The criterion was proposed, not because teachers are less effective than other components of an instructional system, but because there is a need to free teachers for more "significant" activities.

It has long been the writer's conviction that the traditional pattern of teaching makes its greatest demands on the less well developed talents of teachers. Conversely, the traditional pattern reduces opportunities for teachers to do the things they do best. Lecturing, spontaneously writing or drawing on the blackboard, giving demonstrations, and so forth, are not skills at which most teachers are proficient. On the other hand, most teachers appear quite adept at tutoring students with learning difficulties, using personal-social reinforcers, diagnosing learning difficulties, and providing a social model for students. These are some of the "significant" activities to which the writer alluded.

In implementing an instructional system the teacher typically performs a series of functions that are not specified by the system itself. There are, for example, requirements to:

1. Arrange physical facilities
2. Procure adequate supplies and equipment
3. Manage the classroom
4. Respond to individual pupils with learning problems
5. Identify and care for students with health problems
6. Enforce safety rules
7. Communicate with parents
8. Collaborate with fellow teachers, aides, etc.
9. Consult with specialists (speech therapists, psychologists, social workers, etc.)
10. Supervise playground activities, free time, etc.

Only selected ones of these functions will be considered here, those which relate most directly to implementation of the instructional system.[1]

Arranging Physical Facilities

As development of learning tasks is completed, a notation should be made as to the facilities required for each task and the amount of time learners will probably spend using the facilities.

Possibly the first step in planning the physical arrangements is to draw a scaled plan of the room to be used. The plan should indicate:

1. A space for students working individually in autotutorial carrels. The carrels should be equipped with audio-cassette recorders, small projectors for strip and/or movie films, single-concept movie projectors, and other equipment in more or less continuous use.
2. A media reception room for either small groups or individuals, provided with the same equipment as the autotutorial carrels, to be used by small groups of individuals working on some task.
3. Project work-areas for small-group discussion, planning, etc.
4. Supervised study area with equipment for individuals to use in completing reading activities, tests, etc.
5. A laboratory table, workbench, or other space for more active learning tasks.
6. An instructor's station with desk and chairs for working with individual learners and with small groups.

A sample floor-plan for a classroom converted into a learning center is depicted in Fig. 5.1. This particular plan was based on an analysis of the time requirements for a program in which, it was estimated, students spent approximately one-half of their time in reading, working independently on materials, or engaging in out-of-classroom experiences. The supervised study area was designed for fifteen students working at individual study tables. Approximately 30 percent of the estimated time was devoted to autotutorial experiences, using one or more of the equipment-mediated modes, so five carrels were prepared for students working independently and one space for another four or five working on the same task at the same time. The analysis further indicated that approximately 15 percent of the time was on small-group "project" work and 5 percent on work which required materials to be manipulated. The small-group discussion spaces and the laboratory facility were specified accordingly.

Note that the learning center is located near the media center, which reduces requirements for storage facilities in the room itself. In a practice, the students, having completed a packet of materials comprising a learning task, received a stamped card from the teacher. They immediately presented the card to the media center to check out the next packet. If the next packet required the learner to operate new equipment, training was provided in the media center.

If a school does not have a media or instructional materials center, or if it is not convenient to the classroom, then provision must be made in the facilities design for the functions of a media center to be located in the classroom.

Of course, if the program involves two or more teachers functioning as a team, with more rooms to design, it may be that the functions can be divided differently. One room may be designated for supervised study and the other prepared entirely for autotutorial, small-group, or laboratory activities. The same process of determining proportionate time requirements will aid in estimating how many special-use facilities should be required.

Procuring Supplies and Equipment

The principal task for the teacher in the procurement of supplies and equipment is ordering far enough in advance to make certain they are on hand when needed. All school systems require lead time to complete administrative details on purchase requests. Moreover, manufacturers do not always maintain adequate stocks, and schedules for the use of films are often made months in advance. These facts

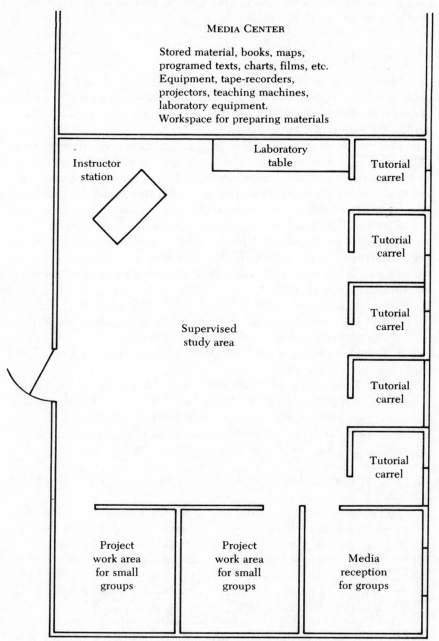

Fig. 5.1. Sample Plan for Converting Classroom into
Learning Center for Individualized Instruction

require teachers to schedule instructional activities well in advance, and then to maintain the schedule.

Classroom Management

The management of events within the individualized classroom represents a different set of activities than the management of the traditional classroom. The first set of functions may be subsumed under the rubric of *coordination.*

The fact that students are much more "on their own" in a program of individualized instruction presents some unique problems of student behavior or may intensify some problems already present. The set of functions designed to maintain an effective social environment constitutes the category of *behavioral management.*

Coordination functions are largely matters of scheduling. It is probably best for the teacher to establish a rather firm pattern of his own activities for each period, allowing so many minutes for each essential activity. Assuming a one-hour period, a teacher might have the following schedule:

9:00-9:10 — available to all students for general questions, obtaining materials, or scheduling work spaces

9:10-9:15 — starting students who have completed tasks on evaluation exercises

9:15-9:45 — moving through study and tutorial areas to consult with individual learners, distribute materials, accept evaluation projects, record student progress, etc.

9:45-9:55 — at desk accepting assignments, doing individual tutoring, and answering questions

As a rule, if students know the teacher's schedule, they will plan their activities to make use of it.

The scheduling of work and tutorial areas represents a more complex problem. It is probably best to prepare a blank schedule for each space and then ask students, as they plan their learning tasks, to sign up for spaces as needed. They will require a week or so of practice, however, before the self-scheduling process works smoothly. The teacher will be of most help in the process by providing reinforcing feedback to the entire group for more efficient self-scheduling.

The fact that students are working more on their own in an individualized program does not *cause* undesirable behavior. As a matter of fact, the careful planning, clear objectives, and frequent feedback will probably reduce behavior problems in the overall sense.

There will remain however, a number of students whose previous development has given rise to short attention spans, tendencies to be easily distracted, patterns of undesirable, inappropriate, or disruptive behavior, or tendencies to shy, timid behavior. It is well for the teacher to anticipate such contingencies and to have plans laid in advance.

The writer strongly urges the teacher to become familiar with the practices of *behavior modification* as a means to solve these problems as they arise. A number of books, articles, and papers are identified in the list of suggested readings in behavior modification and should be studied as a basis for making contingency plans.

The behavior modification process involves:

1. Careful observation of the student's behavior to precisely pinpoint the disruptive or ineffective behaviors
2. Counting each occurrence of the behavior to establish its frequency over a defined period of time
3. Defining a more effective or more appropriate behavior to *substitute* for the inappropriate or ineffective behavior
4. Systematically reinforcing the behavior to be substituted
5. Maintaining a continuous record of increases in the substitute behavior and/or decreases in the ineffective or inappropriate behavior

As an example, consider the case of Mary, a ninth-grader who spends a lot of time "just looking out the window." The teacher makes a record of "window-looking" behavior, checking once each five minutes during the period. In the first week, Mary was looking away from her work seven, five, eight, seven, and six times during the eleven observations made on the five successive days. Apparently, she was spending about half the time "just gazing." As a substitute behavior, the teacher defined all instances of attending to work as desirable, then prepared a chart for Mary with a space for each day of the week for four weeks. She then conferred with Mary as follows:

TEACHER: Mary I have been noticing your reactions to class for the last week and have made a chart of some of them. I'd like to talk about them. I've noticed that apparently it is very difficult for you to pay attention to the work for very long at a time. I counted the number of times I saw you staring out the window each day and it came to seven, five, eight, seven, and six times last week. I'm wondering if I can't

help you pay attention to your work better and make learning a bit easier and faster.

MARY: I dunno, maybe, I just get to thinking and start looking, I
guess.

TEACHER: Yeah, I figured it had been going on for some time, but
we'll not worry about the past. Let's concentrate on the
future.

MARY: All right, but I'm just not interested in school, I guess.

TEACHER: That may be part of it, but probably not nearly all. Tell you
what. I've fixed some cards here that have spaces on them
for each day of the week. I'll keep them at my desk, but
each day when you are here I'll place one on your desk.
Then when I look at you, which will be about ten or eleven
times each period, I'll come over and make a check-mark
in the space for that day each time you are doing your work.

MARY: Why? What good will that do?

TEACHER: Well if I'm right, the whole problem is no big deal, perhaps
just a poor habit you've fallen into. The check-mark lets
you know how well you're dealing with the habit. In technical terms, I'm going to *reinforce* you for a better habit.
We can check each week, or every day if you wish, to see if
there is a gradual increase in the daily total of check-marks.
As soon as you go three days with as many as eight check-
marks, you can take half a period to do anything you like.
OK?

This is an example of a "token" reinforcement system as developed by various psychologists cited in the suggested readings for
Chapter 5. Note that the teacher was specific about the behavior that
constituted the problem. Also, the teacher did not care to just talk
about the problem or its history. In fact she played down efforts to
"explain" it as lack of interest, or as arising from an "unhappy childhood," or any of the favorite explanations that have been developed
to "make sense" of behavior.

Needless to say, Mary's attending behavior *did* increase. And
since it was incompatible with window-looking behavior, that decreased. The rate of improvement was not smooth; there were some
days as bad as any noted during the first week. One might speculate
about those days—asking, Why the regression? and similar questions
—but it would be time wasted. It is better to accept those days, ignoring them as much as possible, and trust the reinforcers to start working again.

The writer is in agreement with behavioral psychologists who hold that much ineffective or inappropriate classroom behavior is due to teachers' inadvertent reinforcing of such behavior. Teachers pay attention to undesirable behavior and thereby maintain it. The processes of behavior modification lead teachers to attend to *appropriate* behaviors and thus to increase and maintain *them* rather than the inappropriate behaviors. As a matter of conviction, the writer considers most cases of teacher failure to be related to ignorance of the principles of reinforcement.[2]

Of course, prevention of ineffective and disruptive behaviors is far better than having to treat them. A variation of the behavior modification procedures will go far in accomplishing this. Simply agree with the students early in the term about what positive behaviors should characterize the class. Post these in a conspicuous place, then praise students on an intermittent basis as they demonstrate agreed-upon behaviors.

Individuals with Learning Problems

Despite careful planning, some students will not make progress in programs of individualized instruction. The same is true in more traditional programs, but such students are revealed much more clearly in an individualized program.

The failures of some of these students are related to problems of ability. In other cases there appears to be a motivational problem of resistance or hostility towards class activities.

Learning ability as a concept is not particularly useful in individualized instruction, so there is seldom reason to begin with tests as a means to diagnose the reasons for a *student's* failure to progress. The diagnosis, rather, should first be of the materials and the design of the learning experiences.

The diagnosis should be made within the context of tutorial sessions in which the teacher reviews the progress the student has made on the task, then has the student explain the problem. The teacher first attempts some simple rewordings of materials, then progressively more cueing or prompting, always attempting to get the student to make a correct response. When, as sometimes happens, the student completely fails to produce a correct response, the teacher may provide it, but then should quickly lead the student back through the process and request him to make the response.

It is especially important for the teacher to note when faster students require tutorial assistance. If a number of fast students experience difficulties on the same task, odds are that slower learners will have trouble also, only more so. If the first group through experiences difficulties, the teacher should take this as a signal to revise task materials or to add supplemental materials that reduce the size of the learning steps, provide more visual cues, increase the feedback, or some combination of these changes.

Above all, the teacher should not overlook the potential in students tutoring each other. Students, when provided with a bit of grounding in reinforcement procedures and in getting active responses from other children (rather than giving them the answer), are able to tutor as well as, if not better than, teachers. Once a student has completed a task, he should be qualified to assist other students if he has a small bit of additional preparation. His original learning will be strengthened by the helping process.

Motivational problems are best treated as problems of behavior management. For students who will not complete tasks, the problem is not in the internal state of the individual — it is in the reinforcement system. The literature on behavior modification offers suggestions on how to identify and arrange reinforcers for such individuals. As a general rule, careful observations must first be made of an individual's behavior in situations where free choices are possible. This leads to identification of his idiosyncratic reinforcers. We may safely assume that activities selected by students at these points are reinforcing. Hence, there is a possibility for contracting the student to behave appropriately in exchange for an opportunity to engage in his reinforcing activity.

A former student of the writer's reported on a case involving a sophomore girl who reportedly "lacked motivation," was "insolent," had a bad attitude toward school, and was failing most of her courses. Whenever given an opportunity, the girl would plop her head down on her desk and apparently go to sleep. The former student simply arranged for her to *earn time* for "head plopping and resting" by contributing to discussions and submitting assignments. It worked. Not only did the girl contribute and complete work, she began to lose interest in sleeping in class. The teacher had, of course, been using smiles and verbal praise as reinforcers in addition to the time for in-class resting. Apparently the *social reinforcers* increased in potency as a result.

The preceding discussion reflects one of the principles of learning expressed in Chapter 1. Secondary or learned reinforcers are highly individual in nature. Most members of a particular culture learn to be reinforced by very similar activities, but there are always individuals who differ, for reasons never well understood. Learning programs must accept learners as they are, using reinforcers that work. If money is the only reinforcer that works, use it. It is not bribery, since bribery involves paying people to violate a law or ethical principle. Paying students to learn (whether in money, personal attention, or check-marks on a chart) is simply a matter of accepting them as they are with their idiosyncratic patterns of secondary reinforcers.

Communication with Parents

Parents can and do influence school learning — probably not as much as popularly supposed, but to some degree. They can learn ways to *increase* their effectiveness, however, and teachers can assist them in such learning. This should be the essential purpose of communicating with parents. For parents of rapid learners, communications should be to the effect that the student has potentials for broadening his learning. Participation in out-of-school experiences in the arts, drama, music, community service, part-time jobs, are all possibilities. For parents of students making limited progress, communications should emphasize the nature of parental activities for enhancing school learning. The emphasis should *not* be on more hours of homework, since these students also require broadened experience. Rather, the communication should be directed toward parents guiding and reinforcing more effective and efficient use of time.

Probably one of the best techniques for teachers to use in working with such parents is communicating clearly the objectives for the program and the underlying rationale. These will need to be "translated" for many parents — stated in terms of actual behavior they can observe and count at home.

The teacher can further communicate with parents on the reinforcements that are useful with children for learning purposes. It is even possible in many instances to contract with parents to use home-based reinforcers to influence school learning! References cited in the suggested readings for this chapter will provide more detailed procedures for teachers on the process of working with parents. The materials are for reading *by* parents as a means for them to develop skills in reinforcing the behavior of their children.

Certainly, one means of communication teachers should not overlook is *progress reports*. Parents, like everyone else, want feedback for their efforts. The form of progress reporting is critical. Such reports should be related to program objectives and communicate clearly to parents the rate of progress students are making in achieving objectives.

Unfortunately, educational researchers have not developed and validated processes for communicating such information to parents. The writer has started a project to test a reporting system based on "mastery of competencies," but he expects another two years to pass before having data on which to report. Teachers, then, will need to experiment on their own.

SYSTEM IMPLEMENTATION II: RECORDING EVIDENCE OF PROGRAM EFFECTIVENESS

System evaluation depends upon good data. Good data provide information about how the system components are functioning—information that is accurate and reliable. Obtaining accurate, reliable information requires a well-planned process implemented by individuals who are aware of what they are doing.

There are literally hundreds of separate observations that can be made on an operational program—so many, in fact, that if a teacher recorded them all, there would be absolutely no time for anything else. To develop a data-gathering plan, then, one must begin by identifying the critical data to be gathered.

It is suggested here that the most critical data are those that permit one to determine the degree to which the system satisfies the thirteen criteria for a good program proposed in Chapter 4.

Space does not permit a repetition of the statements of criteria, nor does it allow a clear demonstration of how measures are derived from criteria. Instead, the writer proposes a set of measures and observations and a means of analysis of data which will answer certain evaluation questions.

A Form for Data Collecting

The task record form developed by the writer to facilitate the collection of data is reproduced as Fig. 5.2. A separate copy of the form is required for each task. Note that the form permits maintenance of progress records for each student (and identification of learning problems) as well as data on programmatic effectiveness.

The first two data columns require the teacher to indicate the beginning and completion dates, which provide the information for computing the third column, "Total Time." The total-time datum

TASK RECORD

Task _____ Number _____ Instructor _____ Subject _____

Student name	Dates		Total time	Number repeats	Requests for individual assistance	Elements for which assistance was requested	Verbal praise given	Behavioral observations										Comments
	Start	Comp.						1	2	3	4	5	6	7	8	9	10	
Totals																		

Fig. 5.2. Teacher's Task Record Form

yields information on *efficiency* of the task materials and, by noting the *spread* or variability among students, whether the task allows variable abilities to be actualized.

Column (4) indicates the number of times individual students have to repeat tasks or portions of tasks to achieve criterion levels. This datum provides more evidence on how effectively and efficiently the materials are functioning.

Columns (5) and (6) provide for the notation of which programmatic elements are ambiguous, too difficult, or just "don't function." The teacher will need to develop a code to use in indicating program elements.

Column (7) indicates the frequency with which the teacher verbally reinforces (1) progress on materials, (2) appropriate behaviors, and (3) developmental behaviors (such as correct speech, active oral participation, cooperation, assistance to other students) set as objectives for individual students.

The next ten columns are used to indicate certain key behaviors over a ten-day period. A code, such as 1 = nonattending, 2 = disruptive behavior, 3 = aggressive behavior, 4 = negative/resistant behavior, 5 = agitated behavior, etc., should be used, with small dots indicating each occurrence. It is probably wise to record no more than two such behaviors during any one task. Others may be attended to on subsequent tasks.

The final column is for noting miscellaneous observations of behavioral responses that clarify the data in other columns or reflect student reactions that tend to indicate their evaluations of tasks activities.

The form in Fig. 5.2 will have to be modified by the teacher if the program is designed to bring students to the point where they are devising larger segments of their own contracts. It will also be necessary to supplement the form with other observations, specified in the next two chapters, which suggest procedures for analysis of data and criteria for assessing indications of the data.

Processes of Data Collection

Students as well as teachers can collect data on the operational effectiveness of the system. Students can rather simply note on a record form included with packet materials such data as: (1) time and date of starting and completing, (2) frequency of requests for assistance, (3) elements for which they require assistance, and (4) comments on and reactions to the task. These data can later be entered in the task record form or compared with the teacher-maintained record.

It is probably best for the teacher to keep the task record forms attached to a clip board and to have them accessible at all times. A form for all tasks on which students are working should be attached to the clipboard. In addition, note paper should be attached on which systematic observations are made relative to conditions in the learning area—such as "No. 3 projector bulb burned out," "Conflict in schedules for laboratory space—three students waiting in line," "Sociodrama in task 24 led to raucous laughter," etc. These observations are crucial for determining the kinds of modifications that need to be made in task materials, facilities arrangements, equipment scheduling, and so forth.

CHAPTER 6

Evaluating System Effectiveness

THE PROBLEM OF EVALUATION

From the foregoing chapters, it is obvious that implementing or field-testing an instructional system can generate massive amounts of data or evidence relating to how well the system performs at each stage of development. The data, however, are in a "raw" form and of limited use for making decisions about the overall system or its component parts, or about how it should be modified.

The purpose, then, of the evaluation subsystem (to return again to the concept of the development process as a system) is to organize data obtained from the operation of a system as a basis for making judgments about the system. The systems developer needs to know: (1) whether the system as a whole functions as expected, (2) whether each component or element makes its contribution to overall effectiveness, and (3) the ways in which defective components or elements fail in performance.

The observant reader will note that the evaluation subsystem is concerned only with assessing the *effectiveness* of the program, not the *worth* or *value* of the program. Questions of worth or value are important, more so than questions of effectiveness. They cannot be answered with any finality, however, until it is known whether or not the system actually works. In other words, one can only determine whether the achievement of certain skills and understandings by students is of value *after* it is shown that students have actually achieved the skills and understandings and have tried them out in the world beyond the classroom. Evaluation in the larger sense will be a topic in Chapter 7.

To evaluate programmatic effectiveness, the systems developer is required to organize available data and evidence to answer a series of questions about the program and about each of its elements or components. The questions and expected answers (which are used as standards against which operations data are compared) are derived from an examination of: (1) the criteria established for a "good" or "adequate" instructional program, and (2) the philosophical and psychological assumptions that underlay the original planning.

The questions lead to a process of summarizing data and of making relevant analyses of data in ways which permit the making of judgments or decisions. The novice systems developer should not be dismayed about the analysis-of-data step. It does not refer to complex or sophisticated *statistical* analyses. As experience in systems development grows, it may become desirable to utilize statistical procedures. Meanwhile, when the need is experienced as a result of a requirement to make discriminating predictions, the systems developer can "take a course" or arrange for consultation from resource persons who have the requisite skills.

QUESTIONS TO BE ANSWERED IN EVALUATION PROCESS

From the criteria for a good or adequate instructional program we can identify the following questions, which will guide or direct the analysis of data collected during implementations of the program.

1. To what degree are all objectives achieved? The matter of degree refers to: (1) How many learners achieved *all* objectives? (2) How many learners achieved criterion levels (assuming criterion levels are less than 100 percent)? and (3) How many learners failed to achieve criterion levels with repeated trials? The answers to these questions can be readily ascertained from a summary of data that reveal the test scores of all the students, the ratings of projects, and records of behavioral observations for individual students and the entire class. By approaching the task analytically, a separate summary can be developed to assess the effectiveness of each packet, unit, or module as well as of the entire program.

Not so readily obtained is a set of standards against which to compare the data. Ideally, one would hope that 100 percent of the learners would master all objectives in the time allowed—or, at least, that all learners would master a minimum number of objectives. Practically speaking, neither will happen. However, the wise teacher will assume that the system needs some modification if less than 50 percent of a typical group do not demonstrate mastery of all objectives and/or if more than 90 percent do not achieve more than the minimum number.

Regardless of the performance of the overall program, as revealed through the performance of learners, the data for each packet or unit should be examined separately. Any packet or unit that reveals student successes below the criterion levels of 50 and 90 percent should be a candidate for revision.

To assist in determining the revisions that are most likely to yield improvement, it is necessary to summarize learner performance on *types* of objectives as follows:

1. Cognitive objectives
   a. Problem-solving
   b. Principle learnings
   c. Concept learnings
   d. Multiple-discrimination learnings
   e. Verbal-association learnings
2. Psychomotor objectives
   a. Motor chains or procedural skills
   b. Strength
   c. Stamina
3. Affective social objectives
   a. Stress tolerance
   b. Attending or concentrating abilities
   c. Cooperative abilities
   d. Goal-setting abilities
   e. Responsibility acceptance

Summing the frequency of successes and errors under each of these classes of objectives will frequently reveal the design problem and direct the systems developer to appropriate remedial measures. The standard for evaluation of instructional design is not arbitrarily specified for this analysis. The systems developer will probably arrange modifications in terms of some priority.

Thus, if it appears from examination of the data that the learners are achieving relatively fewer objectives in the concept, principle, and problem-solving areas and also in the attending or concentrating abilities, the decision may be to *first* redesign the learning experiences for increasing the length of attention or concentration span and then see if this revision improves the acquisition of cognitive skills.

2. To what degree does the system permit learners to progress at their own rate? This question must be answered by inference from the following data:

1. Evidence that some learners complete all packets or units well before the terminal date

2. Evidence that most learners vary from predicted times in both positive and negative directions

3. Evidence that slower-learning students have repeated some packets and have achieved objectives upon repetition

If the data reveal that there is marked variability in rates of completion, it is safe to assume that the program does encourage learners to proceed at their own rate. If, on the other hand, the data indicate that the learners are progressing through the program in more or less lock-step fashion, then very likely something is malfunctioning. It will be necessary to examine all the other data to make a reasonable hypothesis as to why.

If the data indicate that slower-learning students typically do not improve with repetition, it is highly probable that they have not developed sufficient prior learnings to enable them to use the materials. If this proves to be the case, the teacher will need to develop special remedial units or packets to develop the prior learnings.

3. To what extent do learners exercise options to choose the objectives they intend to achieve? This question may be answered rather directly by: (1) summing the number of students who succeed in completing one or more self-designed learning projects, and (2) noting the frequency with which students spontaneously suggest ideas for interesting learning activities or projects.

If most of the learners do actually complete a self-designed learning experience, and there are numerous spontaneous suggestions as to interesting learning activities, the systems designer has reason to consider the system design as successful. If no students complete a self-designed learning experience or mention any likely ideas, something needs attending to. Certainly there are criterion levels between zero and "many" that should indicate a need for attention, but the exact level is an arbitrary decision that each system designer must make for himself. The components that need improvement are most likely the ones that relate to reinforcement and feedback and to the counseling and orienting functions of the teacher (see Chapter 5).

4. To what extent does the program provide learners with skills in the design and development of their own learning experiences? This question is answered by summing the data on the teacher rating forms which estimate the ability of the students to define a problem, analyze the problem, set objectives for self-design learning experiences, etc., during phase (4). Ordinarily, one would expect all students to reach a (3) level on a five-point scale. If substantial numbers do not, then the reasons for failure must be sought in other data.

5. To what extent does the program specify teacher functions that promote individualized learning? The best data for indicating the validity of the planning of teacher function are found in the distribution of teacher time. In programs of individualized instruction it is to be expected that relatively little time will be spent in speaking, describing, or demonstrating to the entire class. The teacher's log should show a summed record of 75 percent or more time devoted to orienting, demonstrating, coaching, and counseling of individual learners. If the log does not reveal a ratio of approximately 3:1 in terms of time with individuals, it is probably a function of inadequate over-all design — instructor functions have been planned to carry unnecessary responsibilities and too little use is being made of instructional technology. As a possible reason, the fault may lie in specific design elements, such as in the advance organizers failing to develop an appropriate set. Again, to discern the probable reason for misappropriation of teacher time, data from all aspects of operation must be examined to "tease out" critical factors.

6. To what extent does the program yield gains in skills and understanding, with least cost per unit-gain? In today's cost-conscious world, this is likely to be considered one of the most critical measures of efficiency. Yet it is difficult to measure satisfactorily. The writer has advocated (without great enthusiasm) that standardized tests be used and that cost-effectiveness be computed in terms of costs per achievement-year per student. The emphasis should be on total or absolute cost with estimates being made of all expenses involved in operating a classroom unit. Public schools usually publish a yearly cost-per-student figure, which can be multiplied by the number of students in a program to obtain a reasonable estimate of program costs. Achievement-years are computed by summing the achievement-test *gains* shown by comparison of last year's scores with this year's. A class of thirty students may then, for example, show forty-three achievement-years, assuming the average gain was approximately 1.40 grade-levels.

There is no rational way to establish a standard against which to compare the per-unit costs of a particular program. If accounting procedures do eventually become refined to the point where costs can be realistically assessed for each objective, then perhaps it will be possible to devise a rational process for program evaluation on the basis of cost. The gain on achievement tests as an index of achievement of objectives is only a gross indicator or estimate. We can, using this index, compare successive classes in a program or make comparisons across programs. In evaluating a new system in terms of cost-effectiveness, one would hope to see increasing rates of gain per unit-cost. There is, however, no available standard to indicate *how much* increase *should* be expected.

If such is not found, if costs remain even or increase with successive implementations of the program, a careful scrutiny of all the data is in order to guess the probable cause. Also, outside factors may contribute to unfavorable cost-effectiveness evaluation. Inflationary spirals, which increase salaries, equipment and supply costs, and the general cost of running a program, will often play a part. Changes in the entry level of students will affect the cost-effectiveness ratio, as will changes in school schedules, policies, and program enrollment. All are factors that have nothing to do with the operational effectiveness of the system.

7. Does the program function within the framework of schedules established by the institution? This question is answered yes or no. If there are frequent reports of individual students failing to meet obligations or responsibilities to other classes, if vacations cause lingering interruptions in the progress of individual students, and if the final part of the semester or program is a mad rush to complete minimum requirements, then the answer is, No!

When the answer is no, the data must be examined to isolate the most likely cause. Data which reveal the time spent on each packet or unit are most likely to give indications of problems.

8. To what extent are school patrons and others satisfied that learning is taking place in the program? The best data here are those derived from ratings of parent reactions to reports of student progress. Using a five-point scale to rate parental responses, at least 75 percent of all reactions (providing there is at least one reaction per student) should indicate that conferees recognize that student time is effectively spent (a three rating on the scale).

Failure to obtain this level suggests that the system should provide increased and/or improved information to parents on both the activities and the progress of individual students and groups of students.

9. To what extent does the program permit efficient use of learner time? The data most useful in answering this question are derived from two sources: (1) records of verbalized complaints by students that they have to "read and reread" assignments, materials, etc., that they have failed to find needed materials, or that materials are no good; (2) records of the number of students having to repeat packets or units to achieve criterion performance levels.

If the data indicate that more than 25 percent of the students complain about a packet being ambiguous or too difficult, the packet or unit should be redesigned, using data from other sources to suggest the needed revisions. If more than 10 percent of a group have to repeat a packet or unit, the need for revision is evident.

10. To what extent does the program provide reinforcing feedback to learners? It is an axiom in learning theory that reinforcement should follow hard on the heels of appropriate behavior. This is so imperative that we would evaluate as inadequate any unit or packet which does not provide a learner with at least three signals of success or mastery per period. The data to be summed for this information derive from records of intervals between successful completion of tests, projects, and other learning activities and a record of the frequency of verbal praise provided by the instructor.

If the summed data do not indicate that reinforcement is occurring as frequently as three times per session for each student, the chances are that the materials are too difficult and do not permit progress to occur frequently, or that the instructor is not attending sufficiently to the cues indicating learner progress. Note that instructor praise and verbal reinforcement should be contingent on *progress*, not on *effort*. If the rate of verbal praise is high and the rate of progress, as indicated by the successful completion of tests and projects, is low, the chances are good that verbal reinforcement is used indiscriminately—for *all* activity and effort, not for *effective* activity.

11. To what extent does the program provide learners with sufficient opportunity for practice with feedback? This question is difficult to answer objectively and with complete satisfaction that the answer is valid. There are no research-based standards to guide one in defining sufficient practice. In general, then, one would judge on the basis of selected performances which are assumed to be the outcome of reinforced practice. In most instructional systems the best indicator is probably the amount of time required to complete tests and other exercises demanding recall of information and experiences.

If the instructor estimates that a particular exercise should take fifteen minutes and over half the learners take thirty minutes, then something is wrong; either the estimate is grossly erroneous or the learners have not had sufficient practice. If observation of students indicates frequent staring into space, fidgeting, or questioning of the instructor with requests for additional cues, the problem is likely to be insufficient practice. Under these conditions a unit or packet should be redesigned to provide additional practice with feedback.

12. To what extent does the program identify learners who do not possess sufficient entry-level skills? From pretest data it is possible to answer this question rather directly: What percentage of the

students who satisfy pretest criteria fail to successfully complete a packet or module on the first trial? If more than 10 percent meet pretest criterion levels and fail, then the pretest is not discriminating enough. Remedial action is either to improve the pretest or to redesign the materials as indicated from an analysis of other data.

13. To what extent does the program encourage the combination of simpler skills into complex abilities which are transferable to out-of-school situations? To evaluate this programmatic quality, all tests and projects must be differentially analyzed to identify instances of *synthesis* of learnings and their *applications* to out-of-class problem solutions. It is not possible to establish standards appropriate to all fields since the learnings differ so extensively. Each instructor must establish his own criteria and indices. As a general approach, in some types of programs where experiences are arranged in rigid sequence, the rate of success in later segments is an indication of abilities to synthesize and apply. In other courses, the evidence must be sought elsewhere — in the home, on the playground, or in the community.

14. To what extent does the program adapt to the characteristics of learners of differing cultural and ethnic backgrounds? All the data collected for the foregoing evaluations should be separately summed for students having unique cultural backgrounds. It will typically be found from such an analysis that materials are differentially effective for various groupings. Urban students have patterns of success different from the patterns of success of rural students. The patterns for minorities are different from those displayed by members of majority groups. From an examination of the successful units, it is often possible to describe the design features that make them successful, and thus to indicate helpful modifications for reducing cultural unfairness of material. In this analysis it is particularly important to examine the vocabulary used, the examples employed, and the differential uses of reading materials and visual-auditory presentations.

PROCESSES IN EVALUATION OF PROGRAMS

The foregoing analyses of data will be expedited by the judicious use of forms to cue the instructor in summing the appropriate data. A form can be developed for the transfer of data from the records of individual students and for each packet or unit. For ease in summing and analysis, a separate page should be used (legal-size is best) for the data providing the basis for the answers to each of the preceding fourteen questions, with rows for each unit or packet in the program and columns for each measure or index. The "boxes" at each inter-section can be used for entries from individual records. A master evaluation form may then be prepared for each unit or packet, sum-marizing all the significant data about that set of materials and indi-cating the priority changes to be made. This becomes the planning guide for materials revision.

A final word about the concept of evaluation. Earlier it was postu-lated that the instructional-systems designer is formulating a hypo-thesis each time he designs a learning experience. He is hypothesizing that specified outcomes will be achieved if the processes he has de-signed are placed into effect. Evaluation is the process of testing that hypothesis. If the hypothesis is not borne out, evaluation guides the formulation of a new hypothesis. Such is the nature of data-based de-cision-making. It is probably as close as education will ever come to making instructional decision-making a truly scientific enterprise.

CHAPTER 7

Final Words

THE PROBLEM OF "WORTH"

Thus far, the systems approach has been presented as a process of controlling and directing the planning activities of a teacher who is solving the problem of developing materials for a program of individualized instruction. The process is systematic in that it provides for decisions to be made at appropriate points. It is systematic also in that criteria and standards are derived from research evidence or from a social consensus and are applied at appropriate points. Finally, it is systematic in that a process of evaluation is built in to provide feedback to the planner, data on which to base further decisions about modification of programmatic elements.

As pointed out previously, the cybernetic features of the developed program do not truly evaluate the work of the systems planner. It is possible to progressively develop a program to a high state of effectiveness and efficiency, only to find that the products of the system are unable to make use of the knowledge and skills they have learned, or even that their knowledge and skills are *maladaptive* when transferred to the larger society.

As examples, consider the following: Instruction in history has, over the years, developed among many students a distorted image of blacks, American Indians, and other minority groups by failing to call attention to their genuine achievements and bona fide heroes. There has been a consistent effort to stereotype the ancestry of minorities through the use of terms like *savage, primitive,* and *peasant* and of descriptive adjectives that confer subhumanity on them. Similarly, the less laudatory actions of the majority groups have been glossed over, ignored, or explained away.

In special programs for slow learners the emphasis has almost exclusively been on developing cue-controlled behavior rather than behavior under the control of consequences — that is, many programs for slow learners concentrate on developing stereotyped responses to selected situations. Thus the "dummy" image is preserved throughout life and there is a continued manifestation of inappropriate behavior. As examples, most such programs concentrate on training retardates to respond to the cues attendant upon entering a work area with smiles, greetings, and an appearance of general friendliness. The writer has observed a number of former trainees of a "special" vocational program continue arriving at work with smiles, loud hellos, and hand-shaking, completely oblivious to negative feedback. The other workers had established the prior pattern of going directly to their workbenches upon arrival, checking over materials, then going to the supply room to replenish their supplies for the day. The retarded employees, with their "greeting" behaviors, were interfering with the other workers, and typically were rebuffed and ridiculed, but despite these consequences their behavior persisted.

Similar behaviors are sometimes noted as effects of vocational training programs. Trained workers resist change; their established behavior in response to certain cues is self-reinforcing and is not under the control of other consequences.

These evaluations are concerned with the relevance, value, and worth of training programs. An evaluation process for obtaining and analyzing data reflecting on the relevance and worth of a system is quite different from the process for collecting and analyzing data reflecting effectiveness and efficiency. This is the topic of the next section.

EVALUATING WORTH

Worth and relevance can be determined empirically only *after* a program has been successfully implemented. *Estimates* of worth are, of course, made during the process of program development. In Chapter 3, a process of utilizing social trends for forecasting student needs was described; the entire goal-setting activity may be conceptualized as estimating worth or value. It is a process by which some kinds of outcomes are predicted to be of more value to learners than other possible outcomes of education. Evaluation of programmatic merit, then, is a process of evaluating the planning process itself.[1]

When and Where?

The purposes of program evaluation dictate that the process occur as a follow-up of graduates. There is no standard specifying that a certain period of time should elapse, but the evaluation should be at a point in time when the former learners are involved in situations where the problem-solving skills are presumably useful to them. A high school program which aims at developing patterns of problem-solving skills for marriage and family living would typically not be followed-up six months after program completion. On the other hand, a program designed to give learners skills in job finding, interviewing, and related matters might well be assessed by data derived from graduates of three months previous.

Obviously, programmatic value is determined from data collected in the actual situation where learned problem-solving skills are employed. Since questionnaires and surveys typically measure responses to questions rather than to life-problem situations, their usefulness for program evaluation is limited. It is probably better to observe a *sample* of a learner group to obtain *extensive* on-site data than to poll the entire group.

Who Evaluates?

This question may perplex readers who are unfamiliar with the variables that influence the evaluation process. The usual answer is, the people responsible for planning the program in the first place. As will be seen, this answer is unsatisfactory.

It is almost axiomatic that the program planner has a vested interest in the success of his program. He has invested it with massive amounts of energy and thought. He has "bet" that his decisions are correct and that his developmental procedures are valid. The likelihood is that his investment will so blind his perceptions that: (1) he may select data confirming his expectations; (2) he may ignore data indicating that miseducation has occurred; and (3) his conclusion-drawing may misassign responsibility for unexpected effects (for example, claiming that the fault is with the husbands [or wives] selected by former students, and not that their learning was inappropriate). Even with an awareness that these factors are operative, there is no way to ensure that their influences are obviated.

The only certain way to obtain objective, valid evaluating is to engage an outside evaluator who agrees to:

1. Avoid entangling personal alliances with planners as a means to reduce the tendency to confirm friends' predictions or to protect friends from unpleasant feedback

2. Organize his efforts to initially determine program goals and objectives from observation and data *without* first reading or interacting with planners on their goals and objectives
3. Interact with planners *after* initial determinations are made to prompt additional investigations to ascertain outcomes
4. Report findings to a wide assortment of audiences and patrons to determine how they weigh or value the outcomes

The use of an outside evaluator, functioning without prior knowledge of program intentions, is consistent with the idea of goal-free evaluation as advocated by Scriven. The reader is urged to avail himself of the items referenced in the list of suggested readings for this chapter as a means to design a more appropriate evaluation scheme.

The typical teacher does not, of course, have resources to employ an outside evaluator, desirable as this may be. How then may the teacher utilize the goal-free approach?

Although there are difficulties involved, it seems best to enlist an interested citizens' or parents' group to plan and implement a process of systematic observation and interviewing to obtain evaluation data and to carry out the other steps in the process. Students may function as data collectors in many instances (with many useful skills being learned in the process). If the school system employs a director or coordinator of evaluation and research, he may provide consultant services to the group, or such personnel may be recruited from nearby colleges or universities. The outside lay group will require some training in the technical aspects of the process, and this must come from either the systems developer or a resource person. Obviously, the resource person is the preferable source of inputs.

The Nature of the Data

It is not possible to discuss here *all* the forms in which data can be collected, so only a few possibilities will be considered. It should be recalled that the primary purpose is to obtain information on how well former students solve problems, not to obtain their opinions about a program. The latter data are more easily obtained and are therefore most often sought in follow-up studies. However, they do not allow a determination of actual performance in the life situation.[2]

Actual performance data may be obtained from many and varied sources. Reports of actual responses to problems may be elicited from teachers, supervisors, friends, and family members. Efforts should be made to contact a variety of observers of former students and inquire as to roughly similar kinds of typical responses. As examples. How does _____ react when he is faced with a deadline? What does _____ do when being reprimanded or criticized? How many times have you found it necessary to explain various procedures to _____?

These questions may be modified slightly to relate to work, family, or community-participation activities. The answers will provide an indication of the generalizability of the skills and understandings developed during an educational or training program. The total range of questions (or probes) will be based on the initial experiences of the evaluators and will be modified as the evaluation proceeds. Respondents will spontaneously add observations to prompt the modifications.

THE FINAL FINAL-WORD: ORGANIZATION FOR FOLLOWING A SYSTEMS APPROACH

The reactions of many readers at this point must be—"So much work." "How on earth can one teacher possibly even *hope* to do all that?"

Yes, it does involve a lot of work and time. It also involves plenty of frustrations, especially as one is beginning to learn to apply the systems approach. Many first efforts come to naught, and the systems approach has a way of making some mistakes glaringly obvious—as, for example, when one prepares a set of objectives that do not lend themselves to programmatic planning and the goal analysis must be redone. In other words, the process can actually be punishing. When work and effort are crowned with failure, one usually tries to avoid the source of failure.

The real problem, then, is to organize developmental processes to reduce errors and mistakes and to provide oneself with feedback that progress is being made.

The forms included in the preceding chapters are useful in this respect. If one starts by scheduling the development process on the basis of completing all copies of each form by certain dates with subschedules for each set of forms, and a record is maintained of progress along the schedule, then one can obtain a fairly satisfactory form of feedback for all the effort on a frequent basis. Most neophytes will notice, as they proceed through each step in the systems approach, that the *rate* of completing forms will gradually increase, indicating in a very real way that skill is increasing. As one proceeds, the quality of production will increase. These are forms of feedback that nearly everybody finds rewarding. Rewards and reinforcement are the best antidote for frustration.

To increase the reward effects, it is often desirable to organize the development process into several miniprojects. After program goals are established, identify the successive subsystems that make up the program. Start the development of the system by carrying through on *all* steps for the first subsystem or unit. Utilize this experience for planning short-cuts or more efficient activities on the second miniproject. Again personal records are important—teachers, like students, require reinforcement. It may be desirable to throw oneself a party each time a unit or minidevelopment project is completed—go ahead—it will be deserved.

Notes

CHAPTER 1

1. Throughout this book *learning* is taken to mean "any persisting change in behavior not due to drugs or to physical injury." Many readers will be troubled by this definition if they consider *learning* to be an event that occurs in the brain or "mind." The notion of learning for them also connotes "improvement." Neither internal change nor improvement is implied by usage of *learning* as "behavior change."

2. There is no consensus on this point. Some authorities argue that learning research (and theory) holds no promise for instructional reform, and that change must begin with revising *instructional* theory and models. In the writer's view, however, these critics overlook the fact that instructional theory and models must be based on some notion (theory) of how people learn. Another point of view is expressed by Cronbach—see suggested readings for Chapter 1.

3. There will always be questions about how many learning principles need be employed by teachers. The writer has usually emphasized seven in his classes, over the years, but he has increased the number to twelve here. The increase is due to dividing some of the seven and adding some which relate to the design of individualized instruction.

4. See suggested readings under Behavior Modification in Chapter 5.

5. Other forms of forgetting are functions of "interference" from previous or subsequent learning. Adequate practice, as advocated in later sections, will reduce such interference. Forgetting in the sense of "passive decay" of learning probably does not occur.

CHAPTER 2

1. This chapter represents a very limited treatment of the subject of systems approach. For a more comprehensive view, the reader should obtain: F. F. Kopstein, *The Systems Approach to Education: An Introduction* (Princeton, N.J.: Educational Testing Service, 1966) or, John Pfieffer, *A New Look at Education: Systems Analysis in Our Schools and Colleges* (Poughkeepsie, N.Y.: Odyssey Press, 1968).

2. See S. W. Hitchcock and W. R. Curtsinger, "Fragile Nurseries of the Sea: Can We Save Our Salt Marshes?" *National Geographic* (June 1972), for an excellent portrayal of a tidal marsh as a system. The article is nontechnical but still does an excellent job of showing the interrelations and dependencies between a tidal marsh and the sea and land and between the living subsystems within the marsh.

3. See Bela Banathy, *Instructional Systems* (Belmont, Calif.: Fearon Publishers, 1968), chaps. 1 and 2.

CHAPTER 3

1. For a description of the educational outcomes classed as affective, see Krathwohl et al., *Taxonomy of Educational Objectives*, vol. 2, *The Affective Domain* (New York: David McKay Co., 1964). For an alternative analysis of affective behavior, see Robert F. Mager, *Developing Attitudes toward Learning* (Palo Alto, Calif.: Fearon Publishers, 1968), chaps. 3 and 4.

2. It should be pointed out, from this example, that no educational or learning method is *automatically* included or eliminated by the systems approach. Any effective method may be incorporated in a system.

3. See John Dewey, *A Common Faith* (New Haven: Yale University Press, 1934) and *Democracy and Education* (New York: Macmillan Co., 1916).

4. See J. M. Adkins, "Behavioral Objectives in Design: A Cautionary Note," *Current Research in Instruction*, ed. R. C. Anderson (Englewood Cliffs, N.J.: Prentice-Hall, 1969). Adkin's criticism of educational objectives as trite and narrow has been thoroughly answered by Eva Baker and W. James Popham in their latest book, *Expanding Dimensions of Instructional Objectives* (Englewood Cliffs, N.J.: Prentice-Hall, 1973). They show how "humanized" objectives can be prepared which emphasize learner processes, abilities, and affective development.

5. Participation by the larger society will have a number of side effects. For example, it will probably lead to increased levels of support for education (engendered by increased levels of understanding of "what education is all about"). The process will increase confrontations, no doubt, but of a healthy kind. Societal participation in educational goal setting is itself an educative act. Members of society should thereby be made more aware of the effects of their present activities on the futures of their children.

6. Robert M. Gagné, *The Conditions of Learning* (New York: Holt, Rinehart & Winston, 1965).

7. M. Woolman, "A Systems Approach to Pre-School Education," 1970. This document, available to the author in the form of a prepublication draft, was prepared for the Office of Economic Opportunity and was due to appear in *Position Papers on Early Childhood Research*. Interested readers should contact the Superintendent of Documents, U.S. Government Printing Office, for the full publication. In the draft, Woolman provided a comprehensive rationale for the use of a systems approach in educational planning, a model for a systems approach, and an example of a preschool system he developed. An excellent discussion of objectives is provided.

8. Stress tolerance obviously belongs somewhere in the S-R and signal-learning ranges of the Gagné hierarchy, and as such skills and understandings are identified, they can be so classified. The point is that the analysis must begin with the world in which the learner encounters stress—not with the higher-level learnings specified by the cognitive hierarchy.

9. Social-skill learnings are, in reality, problem-solving skills and can be sequentially analyzed as such.

10. Robert F. Mager, *Goal Analysis* (Palo Alto, Calif.: Fearon Publishers, 1972).

11. Terminal-performance level involves the area of measurement. Before specifying terminal-performance levels, the systems developer should be thoroughly familiar with educational measurement. Suggested readings from the list for this chapter include the items by Webb and Wood.

CHAPTER 4

1. Some planners of instructional systems would say that the selection of an overall design should actually precede the specification of objectives. However, the design should implement objectives, not control them. As will be seen, *additional* objectives will occasionally be introduced by a particular design, but the decision should never delete or limit objectives.

2. Obviously, these criteria will not be universally accepted. They derive from the writer's personal experiences and philosophy. The point is, the criteria for a "good" program should be identified by the planner or teacher *before* making a programmatic decision. If possible, members of the school's audiences should be involved in setting the criteria.

3. The "purpose" or goal of the subsystem is to select a model which permits identification of specific or unitary learning experiences and the sequence of their presentation. In other words, the model provides a "rationale" for the internal management or organization of an instructional program.

4. Lloyd Homme, *How to Use Contingency Contracting in the Classroom* (Champaign, Ill.: Research Press, 1969).

5. See Myron Woolman, "Training for Adulthood in a Job Corps Center," *Phi Delta Kappan* 48 (1967).

6. The objectives for each element of the process model are "process objectives," not "outcome objectives." Process objectives describe the actions or processes that are to be carried out by programmatic elements but do not indicate what specific learner behaviors will result.

7. The component analysis involves a determination of the worth of alternative components, with a *component* being defined here as a method or technique. A variation of this procedure will be found in Bela Banathy, *Instructional Systems* (Belmont, Calif.: Fearon Publishers, 1968), chap. 4.

CHAPTER 5

1. This does not constitute a complete definition of the role of the teacher. Considerations of teacher role are provided in the suggested readings for this chapter.

2. Read "Why Teachers Fail," chap. 5 of B. F. Skinner's *Technology of Education*, to see how teacher failure is explained by a behavioral psychologist. Skinner strongly condemns the common use of aversive (punishing) contingencies in education and prescribes programming for use of positive reinforcers. His book is included in the list of suggested readings for Chapter 4 under the heading, "Instructional Technology."

CHAPTER 7

1. For a discussion and evaluation of processes of evaluation, see M. Scriven, "The Methodology of Evaluation," in *Perspectives of Curriculum Evaluation*, ed. B. Othanel Smith (Chicago: Rand McNally, 1967).

2. For a brief discussion of the function of evaluation in educational planning, see R. W. Tyler, "Evaluation—The Ultimate Reality," *Educational Technology* 6, no. 18 (1966).

Suggested Readings

CHAPTER 1

BLAKE, H. E., and MCPHERSON, A. W. "Individualized Instruction: Where are We?" *Individualizing Instruction*. Educational Technology Review Series. Englewood Cliffs, N.J.: Educational Technology Publications, 1971. A quick review of status and issues in individualization of instruction.

CRONBACH, LEE J. "How Can Instruction be Adapted to Individual Differences?" In *Perspectives in Individualized Learning*, edited by ROBERT A. WEISGERBER. Itasca, Ill.: F. E. Peacock Publishers, 1971. Cronbach questions the validity of singular approaches to solving the problem of individualization. He doubts that any single approach, such as a materials-mediated approach, will accomplish the goal. As is consistent with his lifelong effort to devise measures of individual differences, he expects final answers to be provided by a complex process of first "diagnosing" students, then placing them in programs which have been experimentally proven to be effective with learners of various diagnostic categories. The present writer agrees, except for maintaining that a separate test procedure is superfluous. The variety of learning experiences should provide the diagnosis.

HOLLAND, JAMES G. "The Misplaced Adaptation to Individual Differences." In *Perspectives in Individualized Learning*, edited by ROBERT A. WEISGERBER. Itasca, Ill.: F. E. Peacock Publishers, 1971. Holland protests against some practices in individualized instruction. He claims that some programs use tests to keep students working until they pass tests rather than using correctly designed learning experiences with positive reinforcement.

JOHNSON, STUART R., and JOHNSON, RITA B. *Developing Individualized Instructional Material*. New York: Westinghouse Learning Press, 1970. In the introductory chapter of this book, the authors provide a concise overview of a process for developing materials for individualized instruction. They see materials as a means to release teachers from some responsibilities in order to have time for the more important activities of (1) diagnosing difficulties experienced by individual learners, (2) interacting with learners needing help, (3) motivating learners, and (4) identifying and encouraging creativity.

KEUSCHER, ROBERT E. "Why Individualize Instruction?" In *Individualization of Instruction: A Teaching Strategy*, edited by VIRGIL M. HOWES. New York: Macmillan Co., 1970.

LEWIS, JAMES, JR. *Administering the Individualized Instruction Program.* West Nyack, N.Y.: Parker Publishing Co., 1971. In the foreword to this book, Lewis shows the need for individualization, particularly for solving the educational problems of members of minority groups.

MILHOLLAN, F., and FORISHA, B. E. *From Skinner to Rogers: Contrasting Approaches to Education.* Lincoln, Nebr.: Professional Educators Publications, 1972. An interesting explanation of the differences among psychological theories. Somewhat oversimplifies, but shows several clear contrasts. Best for a quick review of psychological theorizing and the assumptive basis for such theories.

NICHOLS, E. D. "Is Individualization the Answer?" *Educational Technology* 12 (1972). Answer is yes—if . . . shows need for more inquiry.

SHARP, G. W. "Individualized Study Programs in the General Secondary School Curriculum." *Individualizing Instruction.* Educational Technology Review Series. Englewood Cliffs, N.J.: Educational Technology Publications, 1971. Provides a brief look at selected programs at secondary level.

TUCKMAN, BRUCE W. "The Student-Centered Curriculum: A Concept in Curriculum Innovation." In *Perspectives in Individualized Learning*, edited by ROBERT A. WEISGERBER. Itasca, Ill.: F. E. Peacock Publishers, 1971.

CHAPTER 2

The following bibliography on the systems approach and its applications to education represents a broad sampling of literature in the field. There are many points of commonality in the writings, yet each writer emphasizes a different aspect of systems building or of systems application. The general principles of the systems approach are quite well established, so the reader may select from the following list.

BARSON, JOHN. "Heuristics of Instructional Systems Development: A Team Report." *Audiovisual Instruction* 12, no. 6 (1967). A good beginning reading.

BOULDING, KENNETH E. "General Systems as a Point of View." In *Views on General Systems Theory*, edited by MIHAJLO D. MESAROVIC. New York: John Wiley & Sons, 1964. A rather technical presentation of the use of systems concepts in examining events.

EGBERT, R. L., and COGSWELL, J. F. *System Design in the Bassett High School.* TM 1147. Santa Monica, Calif.: Systems Development Corp., 1963.

_____. *Systems Design for Continuous Progress School: Parts 1 & II.* Santa Monica, Calif.: Systems Development Corp., 1964. Two monographs

illustrating application of systems principles to the design of an entire
school—do not focus on instructional planning per se but on all school
functions.

FINAN, JOHN L. "The System Concept as a Principle of Methological Decision." In *Psychological Principles in System Development,* edited by
ROBERT M. GAGNÉ. New York: Holt, Rinehart & Winston, 1966. A rather
technical discussion of systems concept as embodying a sequence of
decisions.

KAPFER, PHILIP C. "An Instructional Management Strategy for Individualized Learning." *Phi Delta Kappan* 49 (January 1968). Deals with application of systems principles to problems of educational and instructional
management.

LIBSITZ, LAWRENCE, ed. "Systems Approval Makes Progress." *Educational
Technology* (July 1966). Nontechnical discussion of growth of systems
concepts in education.

ODIOME, GEORGE S. "A Systems Approach to Training." *Training Directors
Journal* (October 1965). Describes applications of systems planning procedures to problems of training.

CHAPTER 3

The following bibliography provides a broad sampling of the literature
on defining and preparing descriptions of educational outcomes. Again, there
are broad similarities among the writers. They tend to agree that educational
goal statements should describe observable behavioral events, and that more
specific behaviors should be defined through a process of analysis or determination of the "meaning" of more abstract statements. It is recommended
that the reader study a broad selection of the bibliographic entries as a basis
for selecting among the alternative schemes.

BLOOM, B. S., et al. *Taxonomy of Educational Objectives: Handbook I, Cognitive Domain.* New York: David McKay Co., 1956.

DE CECCO, J. P. *The Psychology of Learning and Instruction: Educational
Psychology.* Englewood Cliffs, N.J.: Prentice-Hall, 1968. Read Chapter
2 of this work.

GAGNÉ, R. M. "Analysis of Instructional Objective." In *Teaching Machines
and Programmed Learning: II,* edited by R. GLASER. Washington: National Education Association, 1965.

HOMME, LLOYD. *How to Use Contingency Contracting in the Classroom.*
Champaign, Ill.: Research Press, 1970. Read Chapter 7 of this work.

JENKINS, J. R., and DENO, S. L. "On the Critical Components of Instructional
Objectives." In *Perspectives in Individualized Learning,* edited by R. A.
WEISGERBER. Itasca, Ill.: F. E. Peacock Publishers, 1971.

JOHNSON, S. R., and JOHNSON, R. B. *Developing Individualized Instructional
Material.* Palo Alto, Calif.: Westinghouse Learning Press, 1970. Read
Chapter 2 of this work.

LINDVALL, C. M., ed. *Defining Educational Objectives.* Pittsburgh: University of Pittsburgh Press, 1964.

Mager, Robert F. *Preparing Instructional Objectives*. Palo Alto, Calif.: Fearon Publishers, 1962.

———. *Goal Analysis*. Palo Alto, Calif.: Fearon Publishers, 1972.

Metfessel, N. S., and Michael, W. B. "Instrumentation of Bloom's and Krathwohl's Taxonomies for the Writing of Educational Objectives." In *Perspectives in Individualized Instruction*, edited by Robert A. Weisgerber. Itasca, Ill.: F. E. Peacock Publishers, 1971.

Maxwell, John, and Tovatt, Anthony, eds., *On Writing Behavioral Objectives for English*. Champaign, Ill.: National Council of Teachers of English, 1970.

Popham, W. J. "Probing the Validity of Arguments against Behavioral Goals." In *Current Research on Instruction*, edited by R. C. Anderson. Englewood Cliffs, N.J.: Prentice-Hall, 1969.

———, and Baker, Eva. *Establishing Instructional Goals*. Englewood Cliffs, N.J.: Prentice-Hall, 1970.

Tyler, Ralph. *Basic Principles of Curriculum and Instruction*. Chicago: University of Chicago Press, 1950.

———. "Some Persistent Questions on Definition of Objectives." In *Defining Educational Objectives*, edited by C. M. Lindvall. Pittsburgh: University of Pittsburgh Press, 1964.

Webb, Eugene, et al. *Unobstrusive Measures: Non-reactive Research in the Social Studies*. Chicago: Rand McNally, 1966.

Wood, D. A. *Test Construction*. Columbus: Charles E. Merrill Books, 1961.

CHAPTER 4

The following materials will provide the reader with basic understandings and skills in instructional design and materials preparation. The items in the list were selected to emphasize practicality and application rather than *research* in learning or methods. The reader who is interested in research-based literature is urged to examine the bibliographies that accompany many of the readings. As a rule, the authors of the works listed here have provided an excellent service to the student of education by organizing research as it pertains to the solving of instructional problems. The readings that follow have been arranged to conform to the topics treated in Chapter 4.

Program Models or Design

Brunner, J. S. "The Act of Discovery." *Harvard Educational Review* 33 (1963). In this paper Brunner presents his basic argument for a "better kind" of learning occurring through nondirected discovery.

———. *Toward a Theory of Instruction*. Cambridge: Harvard University Press, 1966. A small book written in nontechnical language — especially useful for those just becoming acquainted with the field.

Carroll, John B. "A Model of School Learning." *Teachers College Record* 64 (1963). A good, brief introduction to a process of learning which can be used as a model for instruction.

DE CECCO, J. P. *The Psychology of Learning and Instruction.* Englewood Cliffs, N.J.: Prentice-Hall, 1968. A good, comprehensive, college text; Chapter 1 is particularly helpful.

FLANDERS, N. A. "Interaction Analysis and Inservice Training." *California Journal for Instruction Improvement* 9 (1966). A good introduction to Flanders's scheme for analyzing educational processes. Includes an adequate statement of his rationale and assumptions.

GAGNÉ, N. L. "Toward a Cognitive Theory of Teaching." *Teachers College Record* 65 (1964). A readable treatment of a complex subject—presents a model of instruction based on analysis of cognitive elements of learning.

———. "Theories of Teaching." In *Theories of Learning and Instruction,* edited by E. R. HILGARD. Pt. I, 63rd yearbook, National Society for the Study of Education, 1964. A rather technical overview of implications of learning theory for instructional practice and design.

KELLER, F. "Good-bye Teacher." *Journal of Applied Behavioral Analysis* 1 (1968). Keller argues that teaching in the historical sense is passé! He predicts that the advent of programmed approaches will eventually lead to a complete redefinition of the role of the teacher.

LEONARD, G. *Education and Ecstasy.* New York: Delacorte Press, 1968. Leonard does an excellent job of describing an educational process that leads to excitement, joy, and increased interest in learning.

MOSSTON, M. *Teaching: From Command to Discovery.* Belmont, Calif.: Wadsworth Publishing Co., 1972. Mosston speaks of instructional models as "teaching styles," arranging them in a spectrum ranging from teacher control to learner control. His discussion of different styles of teaching is somewhat limited and fails to recognize the amount of variation possible within each style. For example, in Chapter 6 he treats individualized approaches as though there were only a single, entirely teacher controlled model. Apparently Mosston has not encountered the contracting process with its built-in provision for learners gradually developing abilities to self-contract. In Chapter 9, he does provide a set of procedures for a "self-directed" individualized approach, which is an exemplification of the *discovery model.* A careful examination of the model raises some very practical questions, such as, How does one develop the skills necessary for organizing a discovery learning experience?

ROGERS, C. R. "Learning to Be Free." *National Education Association Journal* 52 (1963). The model proposed by Rogers consists largely of elements of the relationship between teacher and learner. For Rogers the essential goal of all education (as of psychotherapy) is "self-actualization," or personal freedom. The school, in developing self-actualization, must free learners from emotional constrictions to enable them to learn fully from experience. Rogers apparently does not perceive similarities between problem-solvers and self-actualizers, so there is no way to judge how he sees the role of skill development in self-actualization.

STOLUROW, L. M., and DAVIS, D. "Teaching Machines and Computer Based Systems." In *Teaching Machines and Programmed Learning II, Data and Directions,* edited by R. GLASER. Washington: Department of

Audio-Visual Instruction, 1965. Stolurow presents an educational model based on research with programmed learning and with computer-assisted instruction.

TAYLOR, C. W. "Questioning and Creating: A Model for Curriculum Reform." *Journal of Creative Behavior* 1 (January 1967). The author prescribes a process of raising questions and problems to stimulate creative activity as a basic model of instruction.

Audiovisual Materials

BRIGGS, L. J. "Learner Variables and Educational Media." In *Perspectives in Individualized Instruction,* edited by R. A. WEISGERBER. Itasca, Ill.: F. E. Peacock Publishers, 1971. Discusses individual differences and implications for selection of media.

BROWN, J. W.; LEWIS, R. B.; and HARCLEROAD, F. F. *AV Instruction: Media and Methods.* New York: McGraw-Hill, 1969. This book is designed for beginning-level college classes in audiovisual methods. It constitutes a handy teacher's reference for solving problems of equipment selection and utilization, preparation of materials, etc. Describes a systematic approach for development of materials and integration with other instructional processes.

DALE, EDGAR. *Audiovisual Methods in Teaching.* New York: Dryden Press, 1969. A college-level text. Emphasizes teacher development and use of audiovisual materials in classes. Plentiful use of examples.

KLASEK, CHARLES B. *Instructional Media in the Modern School.* Lincoln, Nebr.: Professional Educators Publications, 1972. A brief survey of materials and methods. Somewhat overemphasizes educational television and gives but limited coverage of other audiovisual media.

MEIERHENRY, W. C., ed. *Learning Theory and A-V Utilization. A-V Communications Review,* Supplement 4 (October 1961). This supplement was prepared to further *basic* research in the area of audiovisual methods. Presents papers by six authors who have different theoretical orientations within psychology. Implications of psychological research for audiovisual utilization are explored. This small publication is a good introduction for the teacher to basic issues in the application of theory to practice.

WEISGERBER, R. A. "Media, Facilities and Learner Options." In *Perspectives in Individualized Learning,* edited by R. A. WEISGERBER. Itasca, Ill.: F. E. Peacock Publishers, 1971. The author advocates that learners be provided with options in media, and that the differential nature of learnings also be a determinant of selection of equipment and processes. He provides data from empirical tests of media effectiveness with groups and individual learners.

Instructional Technology

BUNDY, ROBERT A. "Computer-Assisted Instruction: Where Are We?" In *Perspectives in Individualized Learning,* edited by ROBERT A. WEISGERBER. Itasca, Ill.: F. E. Peacock Publishers, 1971. For the teacher who wants to know "where we are" in the technology of computer-assisted instruction (CAI), Bundy offers a concise summary of present practices and issues. The overall tone of the essay is that we still have a long way to go before CAI will be in even a minority of classrooms. Moreover, we are not sure at this point whether we *want* them there, even if they should be both available and effective as instructional tools.

FRY, E. R. *Teaching Machines and Programmed Instruction.* New York: McGraw-Hill Book Co., 1963. A basic college text in the field of programmed instruction. Somewhat technical in nature, but offers very comprehensive coverage of research up to 1962 on all programming variables.

GAGNÉ, R. M. "Educational Technology as Technique." *Introduction to Educational Technology.* Educational Technology Review Series. Englewood Cliffs, N.J.: Educational Technology Publications, 1971. Gagné takes the position that the most important elements of educational improvement are to be found in the technology of instruction, the techniques of instruction, and the systematic knowledge associated with them. In other words, Gagné sees procedures as being more important than hardware.

GLASER, R. *Training Research and Education.* New York: John Wiley & Sons, 1968. For Glaser, instructional technology is process, not hardware. In Chapter 1 he identifies *process* as a development from psychological research. He reviews the basic conditions under which learning occurs, as determined by research, and indicates how instructional technique and technology must incorporate these conditions.

LIPSITZ, L., ed. *Technology and Education.* Englewood Cliffs, N.J.: Educational Technology Publications, 1971. This book is a collection of eighteen articles that previously appeared in *Educational Technology.* The articles are thought pieces rather than technical or research papers. As such, they are essentially descriptive of "where we are" and predictive of "where we're going" as viewed by authorities in the field.

MARGOLIN, J. B., and MISCH, M. R., eds. *Computers in the Classroom.* Washington: Spartan Books, 1970. Through contributions of several papers, the editors present a very comprehensive view of the "state of the art" in the use of computers in education.

OFIESH, G. D. "Tomorrow's Educational Engineers." *Introduction to Educational Technology.* Educational Technology Review Series. Englewood Cliffs, N.J.: Educational Technology Publications, 1971. Ofiesh describes the growth of the field of educational technology and the demands this places upon professionals. He argues for the development of *technologists* (students of a technology) rather than preparing *technicians* (practitioners) as a means for education to more readily incorporate upcoming technologies and techniques (including systems-planning techniques).

PRESSEY, S. L. "ReProgram Programming?" *Psychology in the Schools* 4 (1964). Pressey objects to the small-step learning that characterizes programmed instruction. He advocates larger-step presentations, which permit learners to establish their own step-sizes.

SKINNER, B. F. *The Technology of Teaching.* New York: Meridith Corp., 1968. In Chapters 3 and 4, Skinner reflects on the implications of operant learning theory for the design of educational equipment and processes and on the technique of teaching.

Television Cartridge and Disc Systems: What Are They Good For? Washington: National Association of Educational Broadcasters, 1970. A look at the educational potential of a new line of technical equipment. Projects used in schools and classrooms.

To Improve Learning: A Report to the President and Congress, by the Commission on Instructional Technology. Available from the Superintendent of Documents, U.S. Government Printing Office. Provides review of major methods of communication and uses in education. Proposes establishment of a national institute to solve technical and business problems in educational technology and to encourage development of software to further the utilization of technology.

WADE, SERENA. "Effect of Television Utilization Procedures on Learning." *AV Communications Review* 17 (1969). A comparison of different methods of classroom utilization of educational television. Concludes that effects of educational TV are related to method or technique.

Materials Preparation: Development of Packets and Learning Experiences

AUSUBEL, D. P. "The use of Advance Organizers in the Learning and Retention of Verbal Meaningful Material." *Journal of Educational Psychology* 51 (1960). Helpful information for developing orientation materials for learning experiences.

BURKE, CASEEL. "The Structure and Substance of the WILKIT Instructional Module." *Educational Technology* 12 (1972). WILKITs (acronym for Weber Individualized Instruction Kit), a product of the faculty of Weber State College, Ogden, Utah, are units of work for students in teacher education. The article fully describes both the process by which the kits (or packages) are developed and the completed materials.

CORWIN, REBECCA, "Discovery Boxes." *Educational Technology* 12 (1972). A delightful little article, describing some unique kits, or packages, developed by a childrens' museum. The kits provide an initial structural-learning-activity box in such fields as "Netsilik Eskimos," "Rocks," and "Medieval People," followed by unstructured boxes full of materials to "mess around with" to pursue on the basis of interest.

DRUMHELLER, SIDNEY J. *Handbook of Curriculum Design for Individualized Instruction: A Systems Approach.* Englewood Cliffs, N.J.: Educational Technology Publications, 1970. A very detailed presentation of procedures, rationale, and forms for making the systems approach work.

HOWELL, B. "Tulsapac: Anatomy of a Learning Package." *Educational Technology* 12 (1972). Howell, the Assistant Superintendent for Instruction of the Tulsa, Oklahoma, public schools, provides a description of the learning packages in use in that school system and examples of various elements at different levels.

KAPFER, P. G., and WOODRUFF, A. D. "The Life Involvement Model of Curriculum and Instruction." *Educational Technology* 12 (1972). Describes a model for the planning of educational experiences—a "learning *while* doing" model. A structure is provided for the preparation of learning experiences to develop decision-making capabilities and decision-executing abilities and to interact in five transactional areas of life.

KEMP, J. E. *Instructional Design.* Belmont, Calif.: Fearon Publishers, 1971. The author describes a systematic approach to the development of instructional materials.

LEWIS, JAMES, JR. *Administering the Individualized Instruction Program.* West Nyack, N.Y.: Parker Publishing Co., 1971. In Chapters 7 and 8, Lewis provides a series of guides for the design and production of a variety of learning packets or experiences. Actual examples of the developed materials are provided in the appendix.

POSTLEWAIT, S. N., and HURST, R. N. "The Audio-Tutorial System: Incorporating Mini-courses and Mastery." *Educational Technology* 12 (1972). The authors discuss a rationale for an audiotutorial approach to individualization. They also provide a brief overview of the design of learning booths.

SILVERMAN, R. E. *How to Write a Program.* Carlisle, Mass.: Carlisle Pub., 1970. A programmed text on how to write a programmed text: contains directions for learner to use new skills in actual preparation of materials and for submission to the author for evaluative feedback. Very comprehensive treatment of a complex subject. Good example of a learning package.

TABER, J. I.; GLASER, R.; and SCHAEFER, H. H. *Learning and Programmed Instruction.* Reading, Mass.: Addison-Wesley Publishing Co., 1965. An excellent sourcebook for information on programmed learning and the preparation of programs.

Simulation and Educational Games: Social Learning

BABCOCK, SARANE. "Simulation of a Learning Environment for Career Planning and Vocational Choice." Paper prepared for presentation to the annual meeting of the American Psychological Association, 1966. A learning game in which players progress through a simulated life of career choices and tests of choices. The study is recommended for the beginning systems builder, not as an ideal use of simulation, but because it illustrates how a decision to simulate suggests and controls the design of a learning activity.

KERSH, B. Y. *Classroom Simulation: Further Studies on Dimensions of Reality.* Final Report Title VII, Project #5-0848, NDEA of 1958, Oregon State System of Education. Report of a research project in which teachers were trained in a simulated classroom context.

SHAFTEL, F. R., and SHAFTEL, G. *Role Playing for Social Values.* Englewood Cliffs, N.J.: Prentice-Hall, 1967. Presents a process model for conducting role-playing experiences—tends to emphasize minimum structure and "discovery" by children of mature social behavior. Plentiful supply of examples.

SILBER, K. H., and EWING, J. W. *Environmental Simulation.* Englewood Cliffs, N.J.: Educational Technology Publications, 1971. A small monograph, which uses an engaging format to indicate the dimensions and unique potential of simulation. Not a how-to book, it merely attempts to make the reader aware of how environmental simulation through a 360-degree theater might be useful in achieving some less tangible educational objectives.

TONSEY, P. J., and UNWIN, DERICK. *Simulation and Gaming in Education.* London: Methuen Educational Ltd., 1969. A rather brief overview of the history, present status, and relevant research in design of educational games as life simulators. Chapters 1-6 are most relevant to readers of this book.

Attitudinal Learning

MAGER, ROBERT F. *Developing Attitudes Toward Learning.* Palo Alto, Calif.: Fearon Publishers, 1968. Excellent small book for the planning of experiences to increase approach behaviors and decrease avoidance behaviors. A careful reading of it will provide many ideas on how programs can be organized to increase student interest in learning.

CHAPTER 5

Teacher Function

BANATHY, BELA. *Instructional Systems.* Belmont, Calif.: Fearon Publishers, 1968. In Chapter 6, Banathy provides a brief overview of processes for installing and implementing a system and ways to perform a quality-control function.

HAEFELE, DONALD L. "Self-Instruction and Teacher Education." In *Perspectives in Individualized Learning,* edited by ROBERT A. WEISGERBER. Itasca, Ill.: F. E. Peacock Publishers, 1971. Haefele provides a brief description of the program of teacher preparation at the University of Tennessee. The program emphasizes the role and functions of the teacher as a *planner* of instructional programs and materials.

LEWIS, JAMES, JR. *Administering the Individualized Instruction Program.* West Nyack, N.Y.: Parker Publishing Co., 1971. In Chapter 11, Lewis provides alternative designs for a classroom, and suggested procedures (functions) for the teacher.

SMITH, L. W., and KAPFER, P. G. "Classroom Management of Learning Package Programs." *Educational Technology* (1972). The authors provide an overview of the general management methods they believe teachers should follow in individualized classrooms.

SOUTHWORTH, HORTON C. "A Model of Teacher Training for the Individualization of Instruction." In *Perspectives In Individualized Learning,* edited by ROBERT A. WEISGERBER. Itasca, Ill.: F. E. Peacock Publishers, 1971. Southworth presents what must be considered an early effort to define the competencies required of teachers for individualization of instruction. The teacher who aspires to individualize instruction might well study Southworth's set of competencies and attempt to determine which ones he will need to develop.

Modification of Classroom Behaviors

There are innumerable writings describing specific applications of behavioral techniques to problems of classroom management. The works listed below represent only a sample, though a rather significant sample, of the ones available. Consistent throughout the readings is an emphasis on the use of reinforcement as a means to increase healthy, effective development. Although it is not always specified, the emphasis precludes the use of punishment. Skinner, in his essay "Why Teachers Fail" (in *The Technology of Teaching*, cited in the readings for Chapter 4), points out the problems to which the use of punishment gives rise. The reader, when reading the following documents, should ask himself, What would I have done as a teacher if the experimental behaviors described here were manifested in my classroom? The chances are great that most teachers would *suppress* inappropriate behaviors through some form of punishment or aversive contingency. The reader, by making this discrimination at the time of reading, should be somewhat better prepared to experiment with the procedures described in the articles.

BANDURA, A. "Behavior Modification through Modeling Procedures." In *Research in Behavior Modification*, edited by ULLMAN L. KRASNER. New York: Holt, Rinehart & Winston, 1965.

BARRISH, H.; SAUNDERS, M.; and WOLF, M. M. "Good Behavior Game: Effects of Individual Contingencies on Disruptive Behavior in a Classroom." *Journal of Applied Behavior Analysis* 2 (1969).

BIJOU, S. "Implications of Behavioral Science for Counseling and Guidance." In *Revolution in Counseling*, edited by J. D. KRUMBOLTZ. Boston: Houghton Mifflin Co., 1966.

BRODEN, M.; HALL, R. V.; DUNLAP, A.; and CLARK, R. "Effects of Teacher Attention and Token Reinforcement System in a Junior High School Special Education Class." *Exceptional Children* 36 (1970).

HALL, R. V.; LUND, D.; and JACKSON, D. "Effects of Teacher Attention on Study Behavior." *Journal of Applied Behavior Analysis* 1 (1968).

HALL, R. V.; PANYAN, M.; RABON, D.; and BRODEN, M. "Instructing Beginning Teachers in Reinforcement Procedures Which Improve Classroom Control." *Journal of Applied Behavior Analysis* 1 (1968).

HARRIS, F. R.; WOLF, M. M.; and BAER, D. M. "Efforts of Adult Social Reinforcement on Child Behavior." *Young Children* 20 (1969).

LOVITT, T. C. "Academic Response Rate as a Function of Teacher and Self-Imposed Contingencies." *Journal of Applied Behavior Analysis* 2 (1969).

_____, and CURTISS, K. A. "Effects of Manipulating an Antecedent Event on Mathematics Response Rate." *Journal of Applied Behavior Analysis* 1 (1968).

MADSEN, C. H.; BECKER, W. C.; and THOMAS, D. R. "Rules, Praise, and Ignoring: Elements of Elementary Classroom Control." *Journal of Applied Behavior Analysis* 1 (1968).

PATTERSON, G. R. "An Application of Conditioning Techniques to the Control of a Hyperactive Child." In *Case Studies in Behavior Modification*. New York: Holt, Rinehart & Winston, 1965.

Books providing more comprehensive coverage of the subject of behavior modification

ASHEM, B. A., and POSER, E. G. *Adaptive Learning: Behavior Modification with Children*. New York: Pergamon Press, 1973.

BLACKMAN, G. A., and SILBERMAN, A. *Modification of Child Behavior*. Belmont, Calif.: Wadsworth Publishing Co., 1971.

MEACHAM, M. L., and WIESEN, A. E. *Changing Classroom Behavior: A Manual for Precision Teaching*. Scranton: International Textbook Co., 1971.

Consulting with Parents

There are a number of materials with which teachers may help parents to become more effective in helping their children become more effective learners, often, in the process, improving parent-child relations. Two, which have been found to be especially helpful, are listed below.

BECKER, WESLEY C. *Parents Are Teachers: A Child Management Program*. Champaign, Ill.: Research Press Co., 1971. A programmed text in the application of behavior modification.

PATTERSON, G. R., and GULLION, M. E. *Living With Children: New Methods for Parents and Teachers*. Champaign, Ill.: Research Press Co., 1968. A quasi-programmed text which provides parents with procedures for helping their child in learning. Good introduction to behavioral techniques.

CHAPTER 6

CARBONE, R. F. "Criteria for Evaluating a Non-Graded School." *Individualizing Instruction*. Educational Technology Review Series. Englewood Cliffs, N.J.: Educational Technology Publications, 1971. Carbone develops forty-three criteria for evaluation of all aspects of a nongraded school utilizing individualized approaches. The criteria tend to be rather ambiguous at times, such as "Teachers make a serious effort to individualize instruction." The reader will need to operationalize the criteria. A good introductory reading; illustrates many criteria not mentioned in Chapter 6.

JOHNSON, STUART, and JOHNSON, RITA. *Developing Individualized Instructional Materials*. New York: Westinghouse Learning Press, 1970. In Chapter 5 the Johnsons present a scheme for evaluating instructional materials that utilizes error rate, diagnostic tests, measures of response latency, a measure to determine whether all materials are needed (the "black-out" approach), and an interview procedure to determine changes that should be made in programs.

LEWIS, JAMES, JR. *Administering the Individualized Instruction Program*. West Nyack, N.Y.: Parker Publishing Co., 1971. In Chapter 10, "Evaluating the Individualized Instruction Program," Lewis provides a general procedure and suggested forms for program evaluation.

MAGER, ROBERT F., and PIPE, PETER. *Analyzing Performance Problems*. Belmont, Calif.: Fearon Publishers, 1970. The authors present a scheme for analyzing the learning problems of individual students. The scheme involves procedures for asking a series of questions about the performance of an individual. The same questions, if developed into a form to cue the teacher, can be used to partially evaluate program effectiveness since we depend on group data to inform us of overall programmatic effects. A very useful book. Tends to remove much of the mystery from educational diagnosis.

SKINNER, B. F. *The Technology of Teaching*. New York: Meridith Corp., 1968. Read Chapters 1, 2, 5, and 9.

STAKE, R. "The Countenance of Educational Evaluation." *Teachers College Record* 68, no. 7 (1967). An overview, at a somewhat advanced level, of a theory of educational evaluation.

WEISGERBER, ROBERT A., ed. *Perspectives in Individualized Learning*. Itasca, Ill.: F. E. Peacock Publishers, 1971. Part F, "Evaluation: The Key to Improving the Learning Environment," comprises three papers. The first, by Gabriel Della-Piana and his associates, suggests a sequential procedure for evaluation which provides systematic comparisons with alternative procedures. The second, by Paul Richard and Robert B. Sund, reports on the use of a questionnaire to probe student reactions to an individualized biology course. It does not deal with the issues present in this type of evaluation and simply offers an example of one evaluation of this type. In the third paper, Richard L. Jenks presents a conceptual plan for evaluating programs in small school districts.